WOMEN OF THE COVENANT

The Case for Female
Roman Catholic Priests

By

Sally Moran

Sally Moran

Nov 04

ISBN: 1-4107-7255-1 (e-book)
ISBN: 1-4107-7254-3 (Paperback)

Library of Congress Control Number: 2003095472

This book is printed on acid free paper.

Printed in the United States of America
Bloomington, IN

1stBooks - rev. 03/11/04

CONTENTS

iii

PART II TRADITION

PART III MAGISTERIUM

PART IV

PROLOGUE

"If only I were a priest…"

Therese of Lisieux
Doctor of the Church

ACKNOWLEDGEMENTS

My thanks to Rose, who encouraged my early efforts; to Steve, who introduced me to cyber-world and provided access to university libraries; to Anne, whose patience, advice, pertinent questions and critical re-reading of the manuscript motivated me through many months of work.

Gratitude is due also to my family who endured my literary vagaries.

PREFACE

During March 2000, John Paul II accomplished a media coup. Images of the frail, stooped, aging Pope praying at the Western Wall in Jerusalem dominated major television network news programs and national magazines, headlined in prominent newspapers and occupied political analysts on talk radio. His trip to Israel, coupled with his Day of Pardon Mass, sought forgiveness for the "past and present" sins of the Church. Pardon and purification of memory were requested for the Great Schism between the Eastern and Roman churches, initiated in the fourteenth century; for the Reformation, begun in the sixteenth century; for the use of force in service of the truth during the Crusades and the Inquisition, pursued during the eleventh through the nineteenth centuries; for the tormented relationship between Christians and the Jewish people, which existed for twenty centuries; and finally, for the Church's responsibility in the "Evils of Today."[1] Sadly, among this litany of sins, the Pope omitted the Vatican's persistently negative posture towards persons of the feminine gender, maintained from the fourth through the twentieth centuries. In this, the third millennium of Christianity, while Rome proposed reform for the people of God, the Vatican still maintained that the Church cannot ordain women. Yet, more than half of all Christian denominations plus thirty percent of congregations within Conservative and Reform Judaism ordain women. They have done so only after exhaustive Scriptural research, prayer and debate. It is most unlikely that these communities of faith are in error. But, John Paul II, in his Apostolic Letter, "Sacerdotalis Ordinatio", (May 1994) maintained that "the Church has no authority whatsoever to confer priestly ordination on woman and…this judgment is to be DEFINITIVELY HELD (emphasis mine) by all the Church's faithful."[2] His subsequent Apostolic Letter, "Ad Tuendam Fidem" (May 1998) revised the Code of Canon Law and stressed Catholics' obligation to accept and adhere to all Church teachings. Subsequently, Joseph Cardinal Ratzinger of the Congregation for the Doctrine of the Faith, issued a Doctrinal Commentary on "Ad Tuendam Fidem" explaining that 'definitive teaching' must be accepted as completely as 'divinely revealed' teaching.

In 1962, when John XXIII convened the Second Vatican Council (soon known as Vatican II), he placed emphasis on dialogue and collegiality, which presupposed legitimate dissent from hierarchical teaching. Yet, on October 13, 1998, the Doctrinal Committee of the Conference of U.S. Catholic Bishops echoed the Vatican by stating that "Sacerdotalis Ordinatio" must "be held definitively by all the faithful as belonging to the deposit of faith." By citing "deposit of faith" the hierarchy seeks to bind all Catholics in faith, mind and will. Such ideological absolutism ignores the right of individual conscience delineated in "Dignitatis Humanae" which states:"…man must not be forced to act contrary to conscience…especially in religious matters."[3] The Vatican, under John Paul II who eloquently champions human rights, ruthlessly silences theologians, missionaries, pastors, professors, consecrated women and laity who fail to submit to any-and-all Vatican positions.

In referring to women's exclusion from ordination, Cardinal Ratzinger stated, "It is founded on the Word of God, constantly preserved and applied in the Tradition of the Church, it has always been set forth infallibly by the ordinary and universal Magisterium."[4] "Constantly preserved and applied", like the words "has always been", are phrases which appear not infrequently in Vatican documents. For example, in the report of the international Theological Commission concerning "The Church and the Faults of the Past", issued in December 1999, one reads, "The Jubilee HAS ALWAYS BEEN (emphasis mine) lived in the Church…from its first celebration under Boniface VIII in 1300…" That date is seven centuries prior to the present time. Thirteen hundred years of history and Tradition are lost in the term "has always been". Now, on the cusp of a new millennium, thirteen centuries of Church history and Tradition are again ignored in the term "constantly preserved and applied" when referring to ordination of women. During the first thirteen centuries of Church history, females were ordained to ecclesiastic office. Yet the Vatican defends its negative position concerning the ordination of women by citing Scripture, Tradition and Magisterium as if these entities truly support restriction of ordination to men...when, in truth, they validate ordination of women.

Rome teaches that Scripture and Tradition are interrelated and communicate with one another.[5] Logically, it follows that a communicating Scripture must remain open to further interpretation. The documents of Vatican II state that Tradition makes progress within the Church with the help of the Holy Spirit[6] so it follows that Tradition is alive and subject to development. The Vatican claims that the Magisterium is not superior to the Word of God, but is its servant.[7] Therefore, the Church's stated position regarding Scripture, Tradition and Magisterium indicates entities which are alive and still in the process of becoming. As such, they are subject to change, development, evolution. Yet, the Vatican currently prohibits Scriptural reinterpretation and presents Tradition and Magisterium (both Solemn and Ordinary) as infallible. Such extension of the scope of infallibility is most unfortunate since it presents Tradition and Magisterium not only as infallible but as constant and immutable. History has proven otherwise.

In another letter issued from Rome on July 10, 1995, the Pope apologized to women on behalf of the members of the Church who have contributed to discrimination against women. The Pope said that after centuries of discrimination, equality for women was now a matter "not only of justice, but also of necessity."[8] Actually, equality for women involves neither a political debate concerning justice nor an issue of sociological or political necessity. Equality for women includes concern for female ordination which in turn concerns the very essence of the human spirit and such spirit's interaction with its Creator. The souls of females are not in some mysterious manner defective, although that has been the teaching of the Church for almost twenty centuries. God did not create a sub-stratum of human destined to be forever inferior to the androhuman. It is preposterous to teach that the souls of females are such that they cannot be called by the Holy Spirit to full sacerdotal function, and it is ludicrous to expect females or males to believe that the Omnipotent-Creator-Sustainer is gender biased.

Aware of the teachings of Rome and confused by the obvious chasm between some Church statements and Church practice, I am one of a multitude of persons saddened by the declared position of the Bishop of Rome. So, like many others, I decided to seek the truth. Alienated by the enforced silence, I sought answers in Scripture, Tradition and Magisterium, the very entities cited by Rome as the basis for the Vatican's refusal of ordination to women. It has been distressfully enlightening, but spiritually and intellectually empowering. For I learned much about Scripture, Tradition and Magisterium. Most of the knowledge which I acquired is known to Scriptural scholars and theologians. But it is certainly not known by Everywoman in the pew nor by the great majority of faithful, church going, active Catholics, female or male, nor is it known to thousands of disaffected former Roman Catholics.

Hence, this book. It is divided into three parts: Scripture, Tradition and Magisterium.

The Scriptures, which were written mostly by men, and may have been intended, originally, to be read by men, record a YHWH Who spoke with women; patriarchs, prophets and kings whose lives were saved by women; a Covenant which was preserved by women, despite the recurrent profligacy of men. From the Matriarch, Sarah, to the prophet, Anna, the Scriptures are replete with indications from YHWH which endorse, even mandate, priesthood for both genders. One does not need to indulge in hermeneutical ventriloquism in order to find this data.[9]

In the New Testament, Jesus, through His human nature, miracles and teaching, refutes the male subordination of women. The women of Jesus' company of disciples fulfill the elements of Apostleship as defined by Jesus, Peter and the Church. Scripture supports at least two female apostles. Even Paul, despite negative criticism and interpretation throughout the years, did not exclude women from full sacerdotal service. In fact, he worked and shared ministry with females and praised their contributions to Christianity.

Tradition is not the uninterrupted phenomenon claimed by the Vatican. It has been interrupted, repeatedly, sometimes violently. Its history is perverted, hidden. In my search, I discovered evidence that women were ordained, taught, preached, heard confessions, convened synods and administered episcopal sees for many centuries until their rights were abrogated by Papal interdict.

xiv

Like Tradition, Magisterium is not constant. Many teachings, especially those concerning women, changed throughout history. For many centuries, the hierarchy of the Christian Church taught that women were deficient. Fathers of the Church, Doctors of the Church, and Canon Law alleged that women were not in the image of God; were in a perpetual state of subjection; were occasional and incomplete beings and constituted a source of evil. That stance has been reversed only within the last fifty years!

Since the fourth century, Rome repeatedly censored, silenced, exiled, and in many cases, executed honest, capable, credentialed theologians, scholars, clergy and consecrated women. As recently as May 1996, an American bishop invoked excommunication of hundreds of Catholics in order to silence sincere dissent.

I am not a member of the Church hierarchy. I cannot read Aramaic or Hebrew. My command of Latin and Greek is adequate. But, such lack of specific credentials makes me more representative of the multitudes of Catholic females who are subjected to Vatican discrimination professionally, politically, and most painfully, spiritually. In spite of my limitations, my search has confirmed several essential truths.

Primary among the truths is this: mere apologies from Rome will never suffice and repeated attempts to silence the Church will never succeed. Despite John Paul's ban, over fifty delegates from eleven countries met in London in January 1996 to urge reform. Over two million three hundred thousand persons from Austria and Germany signed petitions urging Church reform. Similar petitions from Slovenia, Switzerland, Belgium, Italy, France and Australia were collected. Both Poland and Ireland, considered to be 'Catholic' countries, rejected Rome in recent political elections. Evidently, the people of God - who are Church - are speaking, loudly and clearly. The cry for reform comes not only from lay persons but from consecrated women and men, deacons, priests, bishops, archbishops, cardinals. Archbishop J.R. Quinn, at Oxford in June 1996, called for a new ecumenical council and sweeping reform of the Vatican.[10] Disagreement among Cardinals has entered the public arena. The late Joseph Cardinal Bernardin, when calling for a project to explore

Catholic Common Ground, evoked both praise and consternation from his peers.

As Pierre Teilhard de Chardin, S.J. (1881-1955), a silenced, exiled theologian, philosopher and scientist said, "The best guarantee that a thing should happen is that it appears to us as vitally necessary."[11] In view of the groundswell of Catholic Christians crying out for renewal, it would appear that Chardin's comment is not only relevant but prophetic.

There are scholars and feminists who believe that a religion which teaches that females are not in God's image has no place for women. But rejection of Roman Catholic Christianity is not the answer. Because I discovered another truth: Jesus/God, via His birth, miracles, teachings and death, utilized a gender specific symbol to demonstrate to "incredulous and obstinate"[12] males that women are commissioned to full ordained ministry. Unlike YHWH, Who selected gender neutral symbols (fire, thunder, lightning) when communicating with humankind, Jesus selected to enter time via the female birth canal. Jesus emerged into humanity covered with amniotic fluid: water and blood. Thus Jesus lifted femaleness above ritual uncleanness to sacramental reverence. Everyday, at every altar within Catholic Christianity, the male priest pours water into the wine before consecrating. Every Eucharist utilizes the feminine symbol selected by Jesus: water and blood.

In Chapter twenty-two of Revelation, the writer describes the trees of life which bear crops, "One in each month."[13] These trees are symbolic of a feminine function, menstruation, which occurs once in each month. The following passage states, "The ban will be lifted"[14]. Is this Scriptural prophecy concerning female ordination?

Christ's mandate to Mary of Magdala, "Go and tell your brethren"[15] constitutes an apostolic mission equal to and previous to His mandate, "Go and make disciples of all nations."[16]

PART I

SCRIPTURE

Sally Moran

INTRODUCTION

Through thousands of years of oral tradition, each ancient culture repeated the old stories for succeeding generations. Families sitting around tribal fires, shepherds resting beneath a starlit sky, children nodding off to sleep in yurtas listened to shamans, elders, crones telling and retelling the tales of their antecedents. Eventually many cultures developed symbolic systems (alphabets) for converting oral traditions to written records. Prayers, chants, creation myths, sagas, sacred truths, history, customs, ethics were included. These records became the sacred books of major faiths: Kojiki - Shintoism, Qur'an - Islam, Sutra -Buddhism, Veda - Hinduism. The Books of the Bible are the partially shared Scripture for Judaism and Christianity. The Hebrew Bible, the TaNaKh, consists of the Torah(the first five books), the Nevi'im (history and prophecy) and Ketuvim (poetry and wisdom lore). Christians utilize the Hebrew Bible plus the Books of the New Testament.

The Bible is literature. A collection of myths, sagas, poetry and laws converted from the oral tradition by many authors and editors over centuries, it has been translated into more than one thousand languages and approximately sixteen hundred dialects. The Bible, called the Book of Books,[1] has influenced art, music, literature. The sculpture of Donatello, Michelangelo, Rodin, the compositions of Handel, Beethoven, Bach and the writings of Donne, Milton, Blake are some examples. Societal mores and civil law reflect Biblical teachings, particularly in Western civilization.

The Bible is also history which recounts more than forty centuries of events in the lives of people within a specific geographic location. Although some Scriptural scholars allege that much of the narrative material is legendary, archaeological research supports many of the major events recorded in the lands of the Nile, Tigris, Euphrates and Jordan Rivers and in the countries surrounding the Black, Caspian, Dead, Red and Mediterranean Seas.[2] Contemporary Biblical exegetes claim that the Bible is a compilation of lore devised to teach values, ideals, mores, rather than an actual history of the Israelite people.[3] However, Biblical writers did not record their experiences according

3

to current conceptions of historiography. Rather, Biblical authors recounted their own cultural tribal past under the influences of their particular origins, their philosophies, their purposes. Rather than present an event in strict historic format (quite impossible at the time), the Biblical writers utilized symbolic language to depict the presence of the Creator-Sustainer vis-á-vis the behavior of humanity. Varying perspective is apparent in much of the language of the many books of the Bible. Major influences within the Torah include the Yahwists, Elohists and the Priestly tradition. Yahwists, so-called because their name for God was YHWH (Yahweh), probably date back to the tenth century B.C., whereas the Elohist source, which called God, Elohim, is likely to be from the ninth century B.C. The Priestly source may have originated in the sixth century B.C. The particular influence of the various writers sometimes resulted in different versions of the same event, ie, the Genesis creation myth.

Believed by many persons to be the revealed, inspired word of God, the Bible provides the basis for faith in YHWH and the Divine Trinity, delineates expected behavior for faithful adherents and is a source of comfort and consolation for millions of people. The Bible is a liturgical cornerstone for many rites and rituals within Judaism and Christianity.

Among Christians of every denomination, Roman Catholics are the least knowledgeable concerning Scripture. Within the Roman Catholic Church reading of the Bible was rarely encouraged, sometimes forbidden, until Leo XII (Pope 1878-1903) wrote his encyclical, "On the Study of Holy Scripture". Scripture study was then encouraged in seminaries and in schools of theology. Daily Scriptural reading by the lay Catholic was not actively encouraged until Vatican II (1962-1965). Consequently, Scriptural knowledge for many Catholics is limited to that gained by listening to selected short readings from the Old and New Testaments during the Liturgy of the Word during Mass. For many Roman Catholics, independent regular Scripture reading is not part of their usual practice. Hence, their knowledge and appreciation of Scripture is severely limited.

The first five books of the Bible (Genesis, Exodus, Leviticus, Numbers, Deuteronomy) are known to Jewish believers as the Torah, from the Hebrew word for instruction or law. Christians call this segment of Scriptures, Pentateuch, from the Greek words for five scrolls. These books, once called the Five Books of Moses, were originally believed to have been written by Moses. However, the books of the Pentateuch reflect vocabulary and stylistic components reaching across time from the thirteenth to the fourth centuries B.C., utilizing the talents of multiple authors. The history related in the Pentateuch describes the period usually called the Age of the Patriarchs. Included in the narratives are the sagas of Abraham, Isaac, Jacob, Esau and Joseph. Unfortunately for women, these stories have been read and re-read, interpreted and re-interpreted, always extolling the larger-than-life contributions of the Patriarchs[4] to the spiritual, cultural and historical foundations of the Israelite and Islamic peoples. However, as the succeeding chapters will show, it was essentially the Age of the Matriarchs. The matriarchs Sarah, Hagar, Rebekah, Leah and Rachel, each of whom spoke with YHWH, were essential to the initiation, implementation and protection of YHWH's Covenant with the Chosen People.

Following Genesis, the Exodus Book covers the Mosaic Period including stories of Moses and the trials and travails of the Israelites while journeying from Egypt to the Promised Land. Most importantly, these books also include stories of women who were vital to the Covenant. Thousands of women existed side-by-side with men, contributing to the economy, the culture, the family and tribal life. Most were never mentioned. Examples of unnamed women include the Jewish mid-wives who disobeyed Pharaoh's edict to slay all Jewish male infants, and Pharaoh's daughter, who nurtured Moses. Apparently social class did not influence the literary neglect of women. However, the Pentateuch also includes identified women such as Miriam, Jochobed, Zipporah, who contributed uniquely to the maintenance of YHWH's Covenant. Exodus concludes with the protection of YHWH through clouds and fire for all Israel to see.

The title of the book, Leviticus, relies on the root word for Levi, son of Leah and Jacob, who was the ancestor of Moses and his brother, Aaron. Aaron became the high priest and the Levites, the priestly tribe. Leviticus is a compilation of rituals concerning sacrificial oblations, sacerdotal ordination, festival days. It also contains laws relating to ritual uncleanness, addressing dietary and sexual impurities as well as leprosy. Leprosy was held in such abhorrence that not only persons were held unclean but the contamination included clothing, furnishing, even buildings. Unfortunately, ritual uncleanness contributed to the legitimate subjection of women.

The book of Numbers continues the saga of the Israelites towards Canaan and includes additional narrative concerning sacrifice, festival days and a census of the Levites.

Deuteronomy, the last book of the Pentateuch, includes the ancient and beautiful Song of Moses, his blessing of the tribes of Israel and the account of his death outside the Land of Canaan. It also describes the appointment of Joshua as the successor to Moses. The Book of Deuteronomy has been dated to about 622 B.C.

The books of Joshua through the end of Second Kings (c1200 to 561 B.C.) recount Israelite history from Joshua's conquest of Canaan through the partition of the Promised Land among the Twelve Tribes of Israel. The narrative includes the participation of the prophets Samuel, Elijah, Elisha in the lives of the major Israelite kings. It recounts Israel's decline from a major monarchical power under David and Solomon, the division of Israelites into two nations, the destruction of the Temple of YHWH, the cessation of the Kingdom of Judah. Included within this time period are the stories of several outstanding women: the harlot, Rahab; the judge, Deborah; the prophet, Huldah; the mother of Samuel, Hannah.

The book of Chronicles, which follows 2 Kings, was originally two separate works called First Chronicles and Second Chronicles or First Paralipomenon and Second Paralipomenon in the Septuagint[5] and the Vulgate[6] editions of the Scripture. Chronicles, along with the Books of Ezra and Nehemiah, are the work of one chronicler. Chronicles, which begins with genealogies from Adam to the first Israelite King, Saul, is a repeated, revised hisory of the Israelites, concluding with the decree of cyrus, King of Persia (c538 B.C.). The Books of Ezra and Nehemiah continue the narrative including the return of many Israelites from exile to Jerusalem, the rebuilding of the walls of Jerusalem and the reconstruction of the Temple.

Several Biblical books fall into the area called deuterocanonical or apocrypha. The deuterocanonical term originates from the Greek word meaning second or secondary to, and the Latin word, canon, or Greek, Kanōn, for rule. Hence, any Biblical writing called deuterocanonical refers to books or sections of books not considered 'canon'-lawful by some churches.

Apocrypha, from the Greek, apokruphos, means hidden or, from the Latin, apocryphus, means spurious. Thus books called Apocryphal are considered to be of questionable authorship or authenticity. Such books contribute to differences in Scripture between the Hebrew Bible and Bibles utilized by Roman Catholic, Greek Orthodox and Slavonic Orthodox Churches, as well as Protestant Churches. Examples of such books are Tobit, Judith and Esther.

The Wisdom Books include Job, Psalms, Proverbs, Ecclesiastes, Song of Songs, Wisdom and Ecclesiasticus. The identity of the authors of these books is uncertain as are the dates of origin. The Wisdom Books include hymns of praise of YHWH, allegorical parables, lessons concerning the futility of earthly wealth, erotic love songs, adages on morality.

The prophetic books conclude that section of the Bible which Christians designated "Old Testament". The major prophets Isaiah, Jeremiah and Ezekiel accompany the twelve minor prophets in this section of the Bible.

In 742 B.C., Isaiah received his mission to prophesy. The Book of Isaiah includes oracles of doom, of salvation, of condemnation of foreign nations. Isaiah, credited with many references to the Messiah, both as Suffering Servant, Prince of Peace, Mighty God, is frequently alluded to throughout the New Testament.

Jeremiah preached in Jerusalem during the reign of King Josiah and his successors (c628 - 586 B.C.). Jeremiah was unpopular and risked death with his prophecies which include reference to a future King of the branch of David and a new covenant because the original covenant was destroyed.

Ezekiel, the priest/prophet, preached to the Israelites while they were captives in Babylon (c593 - 571 B.C.). The Book of Ezekiel, a collection of oracles and warnings to the Israelites, condemns foreign nations and describes Ezekiel's vision of the future Temple. Ezekiel was influential in Hebrew mysticism.

The Minor Prophets, a collection of short treatises, covers about three centuries (c 753 - c 400 B.C.) and consists of predictions, poetry, parables, and closes with the promise of reconciliation between generations.

The New Testament consists of twenty-seven books: three Synoptic Gospels (Matthew, Mark, Luke) called so because they bear many similarities to one another, as if seen through 'one eye'; the Gospel of John; the Acts of the Apostles; the letters attributed to Paul, Peter, James, John, Jude, the Letter to the Hebrews and the Book of Revelation. Like the Old Testament, these books are the work of multiple authors. They were written over a span of about one hundred years, most likely from c 40 A.D. to c 150 A.D.

The theme of women as bearers of the Covenant continues in the New Testament where Jesus and Paul actively interacted with women and validated the equality of genders before God. Women of the New Testament include prophets, apostles, deacons, preachers and martyrs. Through their direct intervention, early Chrisianity flourished.

Scripture, continually subjected to scholarly analysis and theological exegesis, is an essential element of the Magisterium and contributes to the development of Tradition.

OLD TESTAMENT

Covenant

Circumcise Your Heart Then and Be Obstinate No Longer
Deut.10:16-20

What is a covenant? The word, originating from Latin roots, literally means coming together, traveling together. It is considered to be a voluntary agreement by two or more persons to perform certain deeds. The Covenant between YHWH, Sarah and Abraham is the foundation for monotheism and signifies the beginning of the Jews as a people selected to worship YHWH and to abandon idolatry.[1] The Biblical Covenant, a journey at once historical, physical and spiritual, also represents the individual pilgrimage of every person to find one's fulfillment, one's God. For many years Sarah and Abraham had waited upon the fulfillment of YHWH's promise: a son for Sarah and Abraham. Then one day, YHWH spoke with Abraham and announced the Covenant; "Bear yourself blameless in my presence." It was then that YHWH changed Abram's name from Abram (av-ram = great father) to Abraham (av raham = father of a multitude), patriarch, and Sarai's name from Sarai (lady) to Sarah (princess), matriarch.[2] In each case the name change involved the addition of the Hebrew letter 'hay', one of the four letters of God's unpronounceable holy name.[3] Thus Sarah and Abraham became mystical partakers of YHWH's presence. In ancient times, a person's name was selected with great care since it was considered an expression of the essence of a person or the identification of one's special mission. YHWH used humanity's gender-neutral symbolism, name changing, to demonstrate that Sarah and Abraham co-equally shared a special destiny, a specific task.

Most importantly, YHWH said, "I will be your God and the God of your descendants after you."[4]

YHWH told Abraham that circumcision was required of all the males of his clan, both those born to his clan as well as those purchased (slaves). For infants this rite was required eight days following birth.[5] Circumcision was practiced widely throughout history. During Abraham's time, Egyptians universally circumcised boys between ages six and twelve.[6] Many other African peoples circumcised adolescent males to mark their entrance into manhood. It is believed that circumcision was practiced by Australian Aborigenes, tribes indigenous to the Western Hemisphere and in Polynesia.[7] There are many theories concerning this rite. Herodotus, a noted Greek historian of the fifth century B.C., opined that it was related to cleanliness. Some Jewish writers saw it as a means to channel man's sexual drive.[8] Rabbi Ibn Ezra held it to be 'chok' - a law beyond reason, to be obeyed without question,[9] while others saw it as a painful reminder of submission to God's will.

What did circumcision mean for Abraham's tribe? Why did YHWH demand it? According to Scripture, YHWH demanded circumcision eight days after birth. Before the infant was even aware of the self as an entity, while still helplessly dependent upon the mother's breast for sustenance and security, he was subjected to a relatively painful experience. Subsequently, the boy should remember forever that his parents had dedicated him to serve YHWH, the singular God.

Abraham, with his son Ishmael, and all of the males in his tribe were circumcised following YHWH's conversation with him. Abraham's circumcision culminated many long years' search for YHWH while Ishmael's circumcision may have marked the end of his boyhood.

For Sarah and Abraham, circumcision was the signature of YHWH, the mark of the Covenant, the symbol of God's beloved presence with them and all their descendants forever. For Abraham, circumcision was a physical sign, a sign limited to males. But for Sarah, this rite indicated another dimension, a circumcision of the heart, of the soul. Years later, Moses explained circumcision of the heart, "Circumcise your heart then and be obtinate no longer…for YHWH, your God is…never partial."[10] … "Real circumcision is in the heart - something not of the letter but of the spirit,"[11] is the explanation given by Paul centuries later in his letter to the Romans. There is no gender limitation in either of those statements.

YHWH's Covenant was established between Sarah and Abraham and their descendants, generation following generation.

Each of the women whose stories are retold in the following pages contributed essentially to the maintenance of YHWH's Covenant, the Covenant which Christians believe reached fulfillment in Jesus Christ and His priesthood.

"You are a royal priesthood."[12]

Sarah

Grant Sarah All She Asks

Gen 21:12

It was approximately four thousand years ago that Sarah, with members of her family, migrated from Ur, a Sumerian city in southern Mesopotamia. Ur was a large urban center where merchants traded turquoise, carved-ivory, spices, frankincense, leather-goods, copper and gold. Graceful ziggurats and sun-baked brick houses glistened in the sun. Figs, pomegranates, grapes, dates, olives and apricots grew in the rich soil. The merchants, priests, priestesses utilized cuneiform writing and practiced polytheism, honoring many deities of whom the most important was the moon goddess, known as Sin in Mesopotamia, Thoth in Egypt, and Nana among the Chaldeans. It was a society filled with amulets, potions, incantations, spells and seers. In their religious fervor, people looked to their women who were skilled herbalists, diviners, interpreters of dreams, priestesses.

The world of Sarah's epoch consisted of many different cultures and varied levels of civilization. In Africa, in the Egyptian capital located at Thebes, Pharaohs maintained power over a populace which often participated in civil strife. The Great Pyramids had been completed and copper mining was underway in the Sinai Peninsula. Thriving urban civilizations existed in Kush and Nubia. In southern

11

Africa, tribes hunted and gathered for sustenance. Far from Sarah's dwelling place, belligerent Aryan tribes migrated into the Indus Valley of the Punjab, and Celtic tribes moved northwest towards the area now called Europe. From the Yellow River Valley in China all the way west to the current British Isles, metal-smiths were using bronze for tools, weapons, jewelry. Gold was mined in Ireland. Australian Aborigenes functioned within their DreamTime, while in the Western Hemisphere North American Plains dwellers hunted bison and raised pumpkins. The Incas and Mayans cultivated maize and worked in ceramics.

Sarah's destination was the land of Canaan, approximately eight hundred miles, as the crow flies. The little group followed the river route along the waterways of the Euphrates. They traveled through fertile plains north towards steep canyons and gorges. They undertook their journey during a time of significant social upheaval. Hordes of Elamite invaders, who eventually destroyed the Sumerian Empire, were moving westwards towards Ur. Ironically, Sarah and her family traveled towards lands controlled by the Assyrians, the most warlike people in the mid-East. In addition to Sarah, the group consisted of Abraham, Sarah's husband and half-brother; Lot, who was Sarah's nephew; and Terah, Sarah's father.[1] They never quite reached the land of Canaan. Instead they stopped in Haran, a fair sized town near the upper reaches of the Euphrates, where date palms, figs, olives, pomegranates, cotton and flowering shrubs grew abundantly in the alluvial soil. The family settled in Haran and remained for an unknown period until Terah died. Then, Sarah's husband, Abraham, was instructed by YHWH to leave Haran "for the land I will show you."[2] This event presented a significant change in humanity's usual behavior before its God. Previously, humans had sought to make contact with their deities, conscious of fear, awe, dependency, impotence. Through excessive sacrificial offerings, extensive fasts, use of hallucinogens and elaborate ritualistic performance, humanity's ancestors attempted to speak with God. Now, according to Scripture, God initiated communication with Abraham.

For centuries people have read the Genesis account of Sarah and Abraham. And throughout those centuries the focus has always been on the patriarch, Abraham. Sarah's contribution has been minimized, even ignored. Yet Sarah was essential to YHWH's Covenant with humanity. Scripture itself, through its record of YHWH's participation in the Genesis narrative, delineates the pre-eminent role of Sarah.

Until this point Sarah and Abraham appear to have been urban dwellers. Ur, Sarah's previous home, was the capital of Sumeria. Genesis recounts that Terah 'made' the family leave Ur, suggesting possible familial reluctance to abandon their dwelling. In those times, urban dwellers scorned nomads who "do not know houses."[3] There was a social dichotomy between them. The nomads were demeaned as sand-ramblers without homes or culture. And now, Sarah and Abraham, urbanites, were required to leave their city, their country, kindred and parents' home to become nomads. Perhaps no longer young and vigorous, they were expected to venture forth to an unspecified destination. While they had lived at Haran, the family had done quite well, amassing possessions and people. Surely they had also acquired friends and developed a pleasant pattern of living for the seasons of their urbanized years. But now, all this had to be abandoned.

Once again, Sarah, Abraham, Lot set forth with all their herds, servants, slaves and possessions. Their comfortable home vacated, they urged their animals onwards, pitched their goat-hair tents, sought adequate water, encountered hostile tribes and dangerous animals, while traveling on foot with asses as beasts of burden. Camels had not yet been domesticated, and although horses had been tamed, their use was still restricted to warfare. Like Abraham, Sarah became a wanderer, a sand-rambler. She made cheese from goat's milk, pulled and wove goat's hair or lamb's wool into thread from which she wove garments for herself and others. Her skills included shrewd bargaining. Since nomads did not grow any crops, she needed to barter for the supply of grain needed to make her daily bread. Sarah spent her years packing and unpacking her possessions and housekeeping implements as she journeyed with Abraham from Ur to Haran to Canaan to Egypt to Canaan. No doubt, many evenings she sat outside her tent as the setting sun spread long shadows on the land. She was caught up in the promise of YHWH. She had abandoned her idols, amulets, rituals, spells. No longer serving false gods, Sarah taught other females to venerate YHWH.

Arriving in Canaan from Haran, Sarah and Abraham traveled through the land until they arrived at Shecham's holy place, the Oak of Moreh. It was there that YHWH told Sarah and Abraham, "It is to your descendants that I will give this land," despite the fact that Sarah was deemed barren.[4] Abraham built an altar to YHWH at that spot. Then they moved onward to mountainous land, east of Bethel. There, Sarah and Abraham pitched their tents and built another altar to YHWH. Eventually, Sarah and Abraham gathered their group together and continued stage by stage towards Negeb, traveling from grassland to grassland in search of food for their flocks. Apparently, it was only when the Negeb was hard pressed by famine that Sarah and Abraham moved into Egypt.

Scripture says that Sarah was very beautiful. Just prior to entering Egypt, Abraham appealed to Sarah for protection. Because she was so beautiful, Abraham feared that the Egyptians would kill him in order to have his wife, Sarah, for themselves. So Abraham asked Sarah, "Tell them you are my sister, so that they may...spare my life because of you."[5] What a reversal of roles! The Patriarch seeking protection from his wife...apparently caring little for Sarah's fate at the hands of the Egyptians. And, believing that she was Abraham's sister, Pharaoh took Sarah as wife and showered wealth upon her and Abraham. This arrangement might have persisted for some time, but YHWH inflicted plagues upon the royal household. Scripture does not explain how Pharaoh divined that Sarah was actually Abraham's spouse, but Pharaoh sent Sarah and Abraham out of Egypt. Rather than punish anyone for the deception, Pharaoh allowed them to leave Egypt with all their persons, flocks, wealth. This event demonstrated either Pharaoh's fear of YHWH or the depth of emotion that he felt for Sarah.

After a while, Abraham heard the words of YHWH, "Have no fear, Abraham, I am your shield. Your reward will be great." But Abraham wanted no reward. He, like Sarah, desired a child, an heir. Abraham reminded YHWH, "I go childless" although he had sons by his concubines and other wives. Then YHWH told Abraham that his descendants, numerous as the stars, would be blessed through Sarah, whose descendants would include nations and kings of peoples. YHWH further explained that the Covenant would be established with the son of Sarah who would be named Isaac. YHWH instructed Abraham, "Grant Sarah all she asks, for it is through Isaac that your name will be carried."[6] YHWH was quite explicit in demonstrating the importance of Sarah. She was at least as essential to the Covenant as was Abraham. Without Sarah, there would have been no Covenant. Sarah's first recorded words in Scripture are powerful and authoritative, "Listen now!"[7] Sarah, impatient in her expectation of the promised son, urged Abraham to cohabit with Hagar, Sarah's slave. The resulting child would belong to Sarah and thus become Abraham's heir. But such a plan demeaned Sarah's role in YHWH' s Covenant, accentuating the child, rather than the mother of such child. Then one hot day, Abraham and Sarah had visitors for whom Sarah kneaded flour and made bread while Abraham directed the preparation of meat, milk, and cream. After the guests finished eating, they asked for Sarah who had remained within her tent, as was the custom. She, however, listened and heard the promise that Sarah would have a son within the year. Sarah, long past menopause, laughed at the prophecy. But she conceived and gave birth to Isaac, the son of the Covenantal promise. There was great rejoicing at his arrival. Later his father, Abraham, gave a banquet to celebrate his weaning. Usually, children were weaned at the age of two or three years in that culture. So Isaac was a healthy toddler, running and playing in the midst of the celebration. Sarah loved Isaac and jealously guarded him and his inheritance.

Sarah lived a long life and eventually died in the land of Canaan. Abraham bought a field which had trees and a cave on it. He buried Sarah within the cave. Like Jesus, Sarah was interred in a new tomb in which no other person had been buried.

Sarah, the Matriarch, is the first person buried in the Tomb of the Patriarchs.

Sarah is essential to the Covenant. The writer of the Letter to the Hebrews[8] recognized Sarah as the peer of Abraham by stating, "It was equally by faith that Sarah...was able to conceive." Paul, in his letter to the Galatians explained, "The child of the free woman (Sarah) was born as the result of YHWH's promise."[9] Thus Sarah is linked with Christ, who is the fulfillment of the Covenantal Promise.

"YHWH dealt kindly with Sarah"[10] who was called barren. Scripture depicts many barren women who lived under this negative label which limited their value to themselves, their families and their tribes. But YHWH repeatedly suspended the natural law to demonstrate the greatness of these women and to validate their essential contribution to the fulfillment of the Divine Plan.

Sarah is the original Matriarch.

Hagar

Where Have You Come From and Where Are You Going?

Gen 16:8

Hagar was an Egyptian, Sarah's slave. As a female gentile slave, she held the most menial position within a Semitic tribe, for in Hagar's time, women were bought, sold, traded, given as gifts. They were used for pleasure, as child-bearers or as laborers. Not counted in a census because they were considered to be the property of their owners, they had no rights. Even the child of a slave's womb would not belong to the slave if her mistress claimed it.

Sarah, impatient because her promised son had failed to materialize, gave Hagar to Abraham, expecting to claim the resulting son as Abraham's heir. Her action was not unusual for in that time period such practice was common in Assyria, Babylonia and Mesopotamia. But when Hagar became pregnant she could not restrain her joy. In fact, Hagar became so self-satisfied that Sarah counted for nothing in Hagar's eyes.[1] Sarah, jealous of Hagar, treated her badly and nagged Abraham saying, "Let YHWH judge between me and you."[2] Abraham, caring little for Hagar, told an angry Sarah, "Treat her as you wish." Sarah treated Hagar so badly that Hagar ran away.

But YHWH intervened. Near a spring in the wilderness, YHWH consoled Hagar and told her, "Go back to Sarah. I will make your descendants too numerous to be counted."[3] YHWH's promise to Hagar echoed the Covenantal promise to Sarah and Abraham. Hagar returned to Sarah, calling YHWH "El Roi" which means "God of Vision". Hagar gave birth to Abraham's son and named him Ishmael, the name YHWH gave him when speaking with Hagar in the wilderness. Ishmael means "God has heard."

At Sarah's insistence Abraham sent Hagar and Ishmael away. One cannot determine from Scripture if Abraham freed Hagar and Ishmael. But, Hagar and Ishmael, out of water in the wilderness of Beersheba, were saved through Divine intervention, for YHWH 'heard' the boy crying.

Ishmael grew to manhood, became a bowman and lived in Paran. Hagar chose a wife for Ishmael from the land of Egypt, her native land. As promised by YHWH, Ishmael fathered twelve sons, each a chief of many tribes,[4] similar to the twelve tribes of Israel. Hagar's descendants include many Kings, Sultans and Imams, as foretold over four millennia ago.[5]

Hagar is the Matriarch of the followers of Allah, the name given to YHWH by the people of Islam. The Bani Qu raish, an Arab tribe, consider themselves descendants of Abraham through Hagar and Ishmael.[6] The Bani Qu raish is the tribe from which Muhammad, the prophet of Islam, originated. Many traditions among the followers of Islam refer to Hagar. The Holy Well of Zem-Zem, which lies within the sacred area of Mecca, is believed to be the one at which Hagar quenched her thirst.[7] Although Egyptian by birth, Hagar brought belief in YHWH/Allah, the One God, to countless multitudes of people. Approximately twenty percent of the world's population, about one billion persons, are Muslim.[8] Statistical projections indicated that in the year 2000, Muslims would outnumber Catholic Christians for the first time in history.[9]

Hagar and Sarah are the primary Matriarchs for all monotheists.

Rebekah

Why Go On Living?

Gen 25:23

Sarah had died and Abraham, quite aged, desired to find a wife for Isaac, preferably not a Canaanite, for they were still pagans. So Abraham sent his steward to the land of his kinfolk to choose a wife for his son. After several days' travel, the steward waited with his camels near a well in Nahor's town in Upper Mesopotamia. It was during the time of day when the village women came to draw water. He had decided that whichever young woman would kindly answer his request for water and would offer to water his camels would be the woman destined to become Isaac's wife.

A very beautiful virgin came towards the well, carrying her pitcher on her shoulder. When Abraham's servant asked her for a "little water to drink from your pitcher," Rebekah, for that was her name, offered him her water and said, "I will draw water for your camels too."[1] The steward immediately offered prayers of gratitude to YHWH, adorned Rebekah with golden rings and bracelets, and asked her for her identity. Rebekah was the daughter of Bethul, Abraham's nephew. The family offered Abraham's steward hospitality, while listening to his wish for Rebekah to travel to Canaan with him, to meet and marry Isaac. Although Rebekah's mother and her brother, Laban, wished to detain Rebekah for ten days, Rebekah agreed to set out with the steward immediately. Rebekah's family assented, blessed her, "Sister of ours, increase to thousands and tens of thousands," reminiscent of YHWH's promise to Sarah and Hagar.

Rebekah, mounted on a camel, traveled with Abraham's servant to the Negeb. As evening shadows lengthened, she saw a man striding through the fields toward her. She asked the servant, "Who is that man...?" Hearing that it was Isaac, Rebekah veiled herself and awaited his arrival. After the steward told Isaac the whole story, Isaac led Rebekah into his home, the tent of his mother, made her his wife, and loved her. Scripture says, "Isaac was consoled for the loss of his mother, Sarah".[2] Like Sarah before her, Rebekah was called barren. Eventually, YHWH heard the prayers of Rebekah and Isaac and she conceived. Carrying twins, she endured a most uncomfortable pregnancy. In her distress Rebekah consulted with YHWH, who told her, "There are two nations in your womb...and the elder shall serve the younger."[3]

When Rebekah's time for parturition arrived, she birthed twin sons: the first-born, Esau and the second, Jacob. As they grew and matured, Esau became a skilled hunter, a man of the outdoors, the favorite son of Isaac. Jacob, a quiet man, remained close to home, the favorite son of Rebekah.

Esau sold his birthright to Jacob for a bowl of lentil soup, apparently caring little for the double share of inheritance and the family leadership it entailed. Eventually, Esau married two Hittite wives, a great disappointment for Rebekah and Isaac.

Eventually, Isaac, now grown old and blind, decided that it was time to give his first-born, Esau, his blessing, for death was not far off. So Isaac sent Esau to hunt for some game to make a savory stew for his father. Isaac planned to eat Esau's stew before he blessed him. Rebekah overheard Isaac and sent for Jacob. She instructed him to take kids from the flock so she could make the kind of stew that Isaac wanted, and Jacob, by bringing the stew to Isaac would receive Isaac's blessing. Jacob, however, reminding his mother that Esau was hairy and Jacob was smooth-skinned, was concerned that Isaac might recognize him and curse rather than bless him. But Rebekah had considered everything. She dressed Jacob in Esau's best clothes, covered his arms and neck with kid-skin and placed the stew with freshly made bread in Jacob's hands. Isaac, unable to determine that it was Jacob rather than Esau, ate the savory stew and blessed Jacob.

Some writers have alleged that Rebekah was deceitful and faithless in allowing Isaac to give his blessing to Jacob instead of Esau. But, Rebekah, remembering YHWH's words, "the elder will serve the younger," ensured the prophecy of YHWH and protected the integrity of the Covenant.

Rebekah, fearing Esau's wrath against Jacob, went to Isaac and reminded him that Jacob needed to wed. Rebekah wanted no woman from among the Canaanites or the Philistines, adorers of idols. So Isaac summoned Jacob, blessed him and sent him to the land of Laban, the brother of Rebekah.

Rebekah, like Sarah, was called barren, spoke with YHWH and jealously guarded the son of the Covenantal Promise.

Rebekah, like Sarah, is a Matriarch.

Rebekah, like Sarah, is buried in the Tomb of the Patriarchs.

Leah and Rachel

Have We Any Share in the Inheritance of Our Father's House?

Gen 31: 14

Jacob, son of Rebekah, arrived at Haran. Again, as in the story of Rebekah, the well used by Laban is a pivotal scene. His beautiful daughter, Rachel, who was a shepherdess, arrived at the well leading her flocks to be watered. Jacob was immediately smitten by her beauty, helped her with the sheep, kissed her and burst into tears. Laban was delighted to have Jacob stay with him and because Jacob worked with Laban's flocks, Laban asked, "Tell me what wages you want."[1] The story of Leah and Rachel vividly demonstrates the male-female relationship within the early Israelite culture, which reflected the prevailing concept of the neighboring cultures concerning women. Women were 'things'...items to be bought, sold, bartered; creatures with few if any rights, intended for male pleasure, child-bearing, labor. Even as wives, they were bought or sold. When Laban questioned Jacob concerning wages, Jacob responded with a price for Rachel, offering to work seven years in order to wed her. Later, when he had 'earned' Rachel, Laban gave Leah to Jacob as wife, explaining that the elder daughter must be wed before the younger. After an angry, disappointed Jacob pledged another seven years' servitude, Laban gave him Rachel as wife also. Furthermore, Laban gave each daughter a female slave as a wedding gift.

In the Hebrew tradition, Leah and Rachel, with Sarah and Rebekah, share the title of Matriarch. Leah and Rachel were sisters, daughters of Laban, Rebekah's brother. Leah, the elder sister, had remarkable eyes. One learns from the Douay translation of Scripture that she was 'blear eyed' which means weak-eyed. However, the Jerusalem Bible describes her as having no sparkle in her eyes, while the New American Bible explains that Leah had lovely eyes. Apparently, Leah's eyes were her only notable feature. Compare Leah's beauty, or her lack thereof, with Rachel. All Scriptural translations agree that Rachel was well formed and beautiful. Apparently her beauty was such that Jacob loved her enough to pledge seven years serviture as a 'bride price'. Evidently, Rachel's beauty negated any need for a dowry.

From their wedding days, which occurred only one week apart, Leah and Rachel became embroiled in rivalry for Jacob's love and attention. Leah, married to Jacob through Laban's subterfuge, was painfully aware that she was unloved and neglected. Initially, Leah hoped that the birth of a son would earn Jacob's love. It is noteworthy that Leah called her first-born son 'Reuben' which according to an ancient source means, "He will love me." Fruitful Leah conceived again and called her second son 'Simeon' meaning, "The Lord heard I was unloved." Again, Leah conceived and bore a third son. Leah, still hopeful, named this son 'Levi' which means, "Now at last my husband will become attached to me." But Leah's ability to provide Jacob with healthy sons was not enough to win his love. One senses some change in Leah's expectations for her next son was called 'Judah' which means, "I will give grateful praise to the Lord." Note the lack of hope for love from Jacob and her focus on YHWH. Scripture says that after Judah's birth, Leah stopped bearing children.

Meanwhile, throughout all those years, Rachel, the beautiful, beloved wife remained childless. Like Sarah had done years previously, Rachel gave Jacob her slave girl, Bilhah, to provide a son in her stead. Bilhah eventually bore two sons to Jacob called Dan and Naphtali. Leah, not to be outdone, gave her slave girl, Zilpah, to Jacob with whom she bore two sons called Gad and Asher.

The rivalry between Leah and Rachel, now more than a decade old, still continued. One day Leah's son, Reuben, found some mandrakes in the field and brought them home to his mother. Rachel, still unable to conceive, pleaded with Leah for some of the mandrakes. Mandrakes (mandragora) was a root herb believed to enhance sexual fertility. But a bitter Leah replied, "Is it not enough to have taken my husband that you should want my son's mandrakes too?"[2] Then an interesting interaction occurred between the wives of Jacob. The scene depicts gender reversal. In a culture where the women were treated as commodities of the men, Leah and Rachel treated Jacob as a sex-object. Rachel announced that after he returned from his work in the fields that night, Jacob would sleep with Leah in exchange for the mandrakes. That evening Leah coldly informed Jacob that she had hired him. Jacob and Leah conceived a fifth son, Issachar, which means, "I have bought you." Later, Leah bore Jacob a sixth son, Zebulun, and a daughter, Dinah. Eventually Rachel conceived a son, Joseph. Her joy was great because God had removed her 'disgrace'.

Years later Jacob decided to leave the land of Laban and return to Canaan, the land of his mother, Rebekah. But first Jacob consulted with Leah and Rachel. Both wives were angry with Laban since he had sold them, wasted their inheritance, treated them as foreigners. So Leah and Rachel agreed to leave the lands of Laban. Jacob with his wives, children, concubines, slaves, flocks and other possessions left Paddan-Aram. Rachel, however, had secretly packed Laban's teraphim (household idols). Laban called the teraphim 'my gods', since he was not a follower of YHWH. These idols were used in divining, in fortune telling. But the idols were also important economically because within a tribe, the person in possession of such images held inheritance rights.[3] Apparently, Rachel resented the loss of her inheritance.

Rachel became pregnant again but died in childbirth while delivering her second son, Benjamin.

Along with their female slaves, each of whom gave Jacob two sons, Leah's and Rachel's offspring were the forefathers of the twelve tribes of Israel. The exploits of the twelve sons included tribal slaughter, incest and attempted fratricide. Yet Leah's son, Levi, was ancestor of Miriam, Moses and Aaron. Leah's other son, Judah, was ancestor of David and Jesus of Nazareth. Rachel's son, Benjamin, was ancestor of Saul, the first Israelite king and of Paul of Tarsus. The names of Leah's sons (for she named them without any apparent intervention from their father, Jacob) portray her emotional and spiritual development. Leah initially had hoped that the birth of sons would earn Jacob's love. But Leah also understood that YHWH was entitled to praise and thanksgiving. Leah traveled from hopeful desire for love and unity with Jacob through contemptuously treating him like a prostitute. Finally, Leah realized that YHWH, the One God, saw her misery, cared that she was unloved and gave her a precious gift. The name Zebulun, given to her youngest son, means 'precious gift'.

Years after Leah's death, Jacob, as his own death neared, directed that he be buried with Leah in the tomb where Abraham lay with Sarah, and Isaac lay with Rebekah. Ironically, the respect and unity, which had eluded Leah all her life, were given to her after death. Leah is buried with Sarah and Rebekah in the Tomb of the Patriarchs.

Rachel, like Sarah and Rebekah, was beautiful, beloved and barren until YHWH intervened on her behalf. Rachel, like Sarah, was jealous of the fertile woman. Rachel, like Sarah, turned from idols to YHWH.[4] Rachel is buried on 'Rachel's Hill' enroute to Bethlehem, where tradition says that Mary and Joseph refreshed themselves at the well near the birthplace of Jesus.

Leah and Rachel are the last of the women called Matriarchs.

Jochebed and Zipporah

She Kept Him Hidden

Ex. 2:3

`

YHWH reiterated the Covenant with Jacob, changing his name to Israel. Israel had fathered twelve sons, forerunners of the twelve tribes of Israel. All of Israel's sons, with their families, went to live in Egypt, where they multiplied and filled the country. Eventually they were oppressed and were treated as slaves. Furthermore, Pharaoh directed the Jewish midwives to kill all Jewish male infants but allow female infants to live. Since the midwives did not kill the male infants, Pharaoh broadened his decree, telling all his subjects to throw every Jewish male infant into the river.

Jochebed was a daughter of Levi, married to Amram, grandson of Levi. Jochebed gave birth to a fine boy-child and managed to save him from Pharaoh's death sentence for three months. Then, fearing discovery, she built a small craft of bullrushes, waterproofed it by covering it with pitch. Before she placed the infant in the basket, she instructed her daughter, Miriam, to hide near the water's edge and watch as the baby floated downstream.

Pharaoh's daughter came to bathe in the river. She noticed the basket, realized the infant was a Hebrew boy and felt compassion for the child. Then Miriam approached Pharaoh's daughter asking, "Shall I find a Hebrew woman to breast-feed him for you?" Pharaoh's daughter agreed. Miriam went away and returned with the infant's mother, Jochebed. When she arrived, Pharaoh's daughter arranged for the mother of Moses to be his wet-nurse and promised her payment for the task. Pharaoh's daughter named the infant, 'Moses', which means, "I drew him out of the water,"[1] and despite Pharaoh's edict, adopted Moses as her son.

Moses eventually became the renowned Law-giver, Leader of the Exodus, one of the greatest persons in the history of Judaism and Christianity.

But Moses, who was raised in the Egyptian court, was hot-tempered. He killed an Egyptian who had slapped a Hebrew.[2] Fearing discovery and prosecution, he fled Egypt and stayed in Midian. While there he married Zipporah, daughter of a pagan priest. While Moses was tending his father-in-law's sheep in the Sinai, Moses noticed a bush blazing with fire without being consumed. Moses was curious about this phenomonen and went closer to look. YHWH called Moses, who covered his face in fear. YHWH explained that the cries of the Israelites who were suffering in Egypt had reached God and YHWH called Moses, "Come now, I will send you to Pharaoh to lead my people…out of Egypt."[3]

But Moses was quite reluctant to return to Egypt where he might be executed for murder. So first Moses retorted, "Who am I to go to

Pharaoh?" YHWH replied, "I shall be with you." Then Moses requested to know the name of the Israelite God. YHWH answered, "I Am Who Am." Again Moses demurred saying "What if they will not listen to me?" And even though YHWH endowed Moses with miraculous powers,[4] Moses then complained that he was a poor speaker, lacking eloquence. He begged YHWH, "Send anyone!" Only after YHWH's anger blazed out against him, did Moses finally comply with YHWH's wishes.

Reluctantly, Moses set out for Egypt, taking with him his wife, Zipporah, and his son, Gershon. One night Moses was in danger of death. The Scripture says that YHWH would have killed him. Immediately Zipporah picked up a sharp flint, circumcised Gershon, touched the foreskin to Moses' genitals saying, "Truly, you are a bridegroom of blood to me."[5] Her swift action saved Moses' life.

One wonders why the son of Moses would go uncircumcised. Was Moses unaware of the Covenant because he was educated as an Egyptian? He did not know the name of the Israelite God, so it seems likely that he was unaware of Israelite lore. Some writers have alleged that Zipporah, a Midianite, would not permit the ritual. This is unlikely, given the lack of power of females at that period in history, in that culture.

Whatever the background, Zipporah's action saved Moses' life and maintained the Covenant intact.

Miriam

Miriam, the prophetess, took up a timbrel, and all the women followed.

Ex.15:20-21

Miriam, elder sister of Moses, a Hebrew girl living in Egypt, was subject to the harsh realities of an exiled people. As a young girl she had exhibited cool courage in speaking with the daughter of the powerful, ruthless Pharaoh. The next time Scripture mentions Miriam, she is described as a prophet. In Israelite culture, a prophet was perceived as a teacher, an interpreter of God's will, a custodian of tradition. According to Scripture, Miriam was well known, revered, a leader among her people.

During the Exodus, YHWH continued to lead Miriam, Moses and Aaron, saying again, "I will be your God." The next time Scripture mentions Miriam, she, with Aaron, is critical of Moses, complaining, "Has YHWH not spoken to us too?" The source of Miriam's and Aaron's concern was the wife of Moses, a Cushite woman. Scholars disagree about this woman. Some maintain that Zipporah had died and that Moses had remarried. Others claim that the Midianite woman, Zipporah, was the same as the Cushite wife, who remained unnamed in Scripture. Now, if she came from Cush, she may have been black, since Cush is identified as being very near Nubia. If she were Midian, she would have been non-Hebrew, an outsider. In either case, Miriam and Aaron grumbled together against the situation. YHWH heard, then called Moses, Aaron and Miriam to the Tent of Meeting. YHWH then explained to them that Moses was special, "I speak with him face to face plainly and not in riddles, and he sees the form of YHWH." [1] When YHWH's cloud retreated, Miriam was a leper, "white as snow". Both Moses and Aaron pleaded with God to heal Miriam, to free her from such corruption. But YHWH demanded that she remain outside the camp for seven days, an exile, an unclean thing. Why Miriam and not Aaron? Was Miriam held to a higher standard? Was Miriam pre-eminent in leadership before Aaron? During the seven days, not one Israelite stirred. They remained in camp and did not leave the site until Miriam was healed.

Miriam was an integral part of Israelite history. Her intervention with Pharaoh's daughter contributed to the safety of the infant Moses. As a prophet she led the Israelites toward YHWH during the Egyptian exile. It was Miriam who raised the timbrel and led the triumphant singing and dancing of the chosen people freed from slavery in the ancient Song of Deliverance, also called the Song of Moses and Miriam.[2] But Miriam is more than that. Some writers see her as a symbol of Mary of Nazareth.[3] She is also symbolic of Woman in the Church of Rome. Perceived to be leprous, unclean, she waits outside the camp. And interestingly, like the Israelites, many in the Church of

Rome refuse to go forward until she is healed and returned to her role as prophet and leader.

Miriam's role in the implementation of YHWH's Covenant is aptly described by the prophet, Micah, "I sent Moses to lead you with Aaron and Miriam."[4]

Rahab

YHWH your God is God

Joshua 2:11

Archeological excavations at the site of the original Jericho identify the city as the world's oldest known population center, dating from about 8,000 B.C. The name, Jerico, may be translated as 'fragrant', although it was called the City of Palm Trees. Two walls, about fifteen feet apart, encircled the city protecting its inhabitants and wealth from marauders. Several buildings, supported by large timbers, were erected over the spaces between the walls. Usually these buildings were placed near the gates within the walls. The buildings served as dwellings, shops and inns as well as look-out posts.

One of these buildings, most likely near the East Gate, served as home and business for the woman, Rahab. She has been called 'harlot' in both the Old and New Testaments. But Josephus and some rabbis called her an inn-keeper. According to scholars, all inn-keepers, considered to be of dubious character, were called harlots.[1]

Joshua, successor to Moses, sent two spies out from Shittim, a region of acaccia trees, northeast of the Dead Sea. They entered Jericho and lodged in the house of Rahab. The words, "There they lodged,"[2] tend to support the role of Rahab as an innkeeper. Rahab was a city-dweller who was active in the weaving trade. Historically, weaving had been performed by women. Looms were usually small and easily transportable so that even nomadic women could weave clothing for their families. But the women who were involved in the

27

textile trade utilized large stationary looms as well as the dyes, fixers and vats necessary for the trade. The fact that Rahab had a large quantity of flax upon her roof suggests that she was a member of the textile trade rather than a professional purveyor of sex, a harlot.

For all its wealth, the political situation in Jericho seemed tenuous at best. Apparently, there was a most active and accurate intelligence network, for the king knew of Rahab's lodgers, knew their objectives almost as soon as they had arrived. The king wasted no time in contacting Rahab and telling her to send the men out to the king's agents. But Rahab had other plans. She had heard about YHWH, the God of Sarah, Rebekah, Leah, Rachel, Jochebed, Zipporah and Miriam. As an innkeeper (or harlot) Rahab met many travelers. She had heard about the Covenant, the Exodus from Egypt, the crossing of the Sea of Reeds. She knew that YHWH is "the God in heaven above and on earth beneath."[3] So Rahab sent the king's men on a useless chase, hid the Israelite men beneath the piles of flax upon her roof, made a pact with them to save herself and all her family. Then she let them down from her window outside the city walls, giving them information concerning the concerns and general outlook of the people of Jericho. She also explained where they should go in order to elude the king's men. Then, as agreed with Joshua's men, she tied a scarlet cord to her window, so the Israelites would spare her and her family.

After the Israelite conquest of Jericho, Rahab and all her relatives were brought to safety outside the camp, according to Scripture. Most likely, they were kept apart because Rahab was a harlot, hence ritually unclean, or simply because they were foreigners. Eventually, the family of Rahab became part of the chosen people because Scripture says, "She has dwelt among Israel until now."[4] By providing safety for the Israelites, Rahab made a major contribution to the maintenance of YHWH's Covenant. Her actions in assisting the Israelites are again recounted in the Letter to the Hebrews, chapter eleven. The writer is stressing the importance of faith. Beginning with Abel, the writer lists Enoch, Noah, Sarah (equally with Abraham), Isaac, Moses and Rahab as examples of faith that guarantees blessings. After Rahab, the writer asks, "Is there any need to say more?" James, in his letter to the early Jewish-Christians, stresses the importance of good works. In chapter two he extols only two persons as examples of faith and good works: Abraham and Rahab. Rahab is one of the four women identified in Matthew's genealogy of Jesus Christ.

Rahab is the first female Biblical character of note who is not identified in some familial relationship with a male. She is self-employed, non-Israelite, yet, like the other notable women, recognizes YHWH as the Supreme God.

Deborah

I will glorify YHWH, God of Israel

Judges 5:3

Within two generations of the death of Joshua (c1100 B.C.), the Israelite tribes reverted to adoration of Astarte and Baal. It seems while living in hedonistic, polytheistic cultures, adherence to the Mosaic Code of behavior was too strenuous and daunting. The Israelites inter-married with non-Israelite tribes and behaved as badly as any of their ancestors. Scripture says that YHWH appointed judges for the Israelites. These judges, followers of YHWH, were persons of honor, rulers, powerful warriors, decision-makers. The judges consistently led the Israelites in the ways of YHWH but the Israelites were almost incorrigible, consistently falling away. In addition to their religious betrayal, they suffered from a loss of civility. So much criminal activity had prevailed among them that caravans ceased to ply their trade among them. Travelers had avoided using the local roads, choosing to move by roundabout routes, hence there was no commerce, no wealth, no freedom among the Israelites. They fell under the influence of Jabin, the king of Canaan, who reigned at Hazor. His commander-in-chief, Sisera, had amassed an impressive army, equipped with nine hundred iron-plated chariots. Such equipment represented the ultimate war weapon of the time. Jabin and Sisera cruelly oppressed the Israelites. The men of Israel were disconsolate and fearful. They were without shields or lances and without the wherewithal to secure them.

In their midst lived Deborah, a well known judge and a prophet. She is the only female identified in Scripture as a judge. Deborah taught the people, listened to their disputes, settled their cases. One day she sent for Barak, the Israelite general, and directed him to lead ten thousand men into battle against Sisera. In view of the superiority of Sisera's arms and the low morale of the Israelites, Barak thought Deborah's decision to be suicidal. He refused to go unless Deborah accompanied him. This was a most unusual scene. The male general, Barak, was fearful, reluctant to undertake battle and depended utterly upon the woman, Deborah. Reminding him that this was the "order of YHWH" she warned him, "I will go with you but the glory will not be yours since YHWH will deliver Sisera into the hands of a woman."[1]

Of course, the battle went well for the forces of YHWH, and Sisera, fearing for his life, ran towards the tent of Jael, wife of Heber, the Kenite. As he slept the deep sleep of utter fatigue, Jael drove a tent peg through his head and killed him. After the battle, Deborah, like Miriam years before, led her people in a great canticle of joy, "The Song of Deborah." Like Miriam before her, Deborah led her people to YHWH. Like the Matriarchs, Deborah preserved the Covenant of YHWH. Deborah's canticle foreshadows Hannah, mother of Samuel, and Mary of Nazareth.

As a result of this victory, the Israelites took heart and eventually defeated Jabin, the well-armed Canaanite king. And the Israelites enjoyed peace for forty years. But, within a century following Deborah's death, the Israelites were again mired in idolatry and self-indulgence. Scripture says, "It was rare for YHWH to speak in those days; visions were uncommon."[2]

Naomi and Ruth

To Whom Does This Young Woman Belong?

Ruth 2:6

The Book of Ruth describes events "in the days of the judges," (c1000 B.C)[1] "when there was no king in Israel, and every man did as he pleased"[2] Famine had exhausted the land and Elimelech with his wife, Naomi, and their two sons, Mahlon and Chilion, left Bethlehem and settled in the up-country of Moab, east of the Jordan. Soon after settling there, Elimelech died. Naomi's sons married Moabite women, Orpah and Ruth. In about ten years, Naomi's sons died without issue, leaving Naomi, Orpah and Ruth. Widows without sons to support them became non-persons, without rights, without any future, soon destitute. But Naomi had somehow learned that Bethlehem's famine was ended and that food was plentiful in the land. So she decided to return to her own people, her own land and she told her daughters-in-law to return to theirs. After significant lamenting, Orpah set out for her own people but Ruth, in a Biblical passage of great beauty which has become quite well-known, told Naomi that she would stay with Naomi:[3]

> wherever you go, I will go,
> wherever you live, I will live.
> Your people shall be my people,
> and your God, my God.
> Wherever you die, I will die
> and there I will be buried

They arrived in Bethlehem, caused quite a stir among the townsfolk, but when greeted as Naomi, which means 'my fair one', Naomi asked to be called, Mara, which means 'bitter' because God "had afflicted" her. They arrived in Bethlehem at the start of the barley harvest. Ruth asked Naomi if she might glean[4] in the fields of "some man who will look on me with favor."[5] Naomi said, "Go, my daughter."

Naomi had a relative on Elimelech's side of the family, called Boaz, who was wealthy. When he saw Ruth, he questioned the chief reaper, "To whom does this young woman belong?"[6] Boaz's question dramatically portrays the status of women at that period of history: she had to 'belong' to someone, she had to be 'property.' A woman alone and independent was an anomaly. He was told that she was the Moabite woman who had come to Bethlehem with Naomi. Boaz had heard of Ruth's kindness and devotion to Naomi, so he welcomed her to glean in his fields until the harvest was finished. When celebration of the end of harvest came with its eating, drinking, threshing, Naomi told Ruth to wash, dress and anoint herself, and after the party, when Boaz was asleep, to lie at his feet after uncovering him. When he awoke, in the dark, he was startled to sense a woman lying near him. He asked Ruth, "Who are you?" Boldly she replied, "Spread your cloak over me for you have the right of redemption over me."[7] She was, in fact, asking him to take her as wife to provide a son for Elimelech's line. Boaz informed Ruth that there was one kinsman more closely related than he who had first right. Right of redemption provided that the closest male relative could buy (redeem) the property of the deceased child-less man and/or marry the widow. The first-born son of the union would be the inheritor of the deceased man's name and be considered, legally, to be his son. The woman was 'redeemed' from her shame: childlessness and widowhood.

The next day, Boaz met the nearer relative and the elders at the town gate. The other kinsman forfeited his right and Boaz pledged to marry Ruth, to keep the name of her father-in-law and his sons in the inheritance so that their names would not disappear from the tribe. Ruth gave birth to Obed, grandfather of David, Israelite king. She brought the baby to Naomi saying, "Your daughter-in-law who loves you and is more to you than seven sons has given him birth."[8] Naomi took him to herself and became his nurse.

Naomi and Ruth are an interesting pair. The elder Judean, Naomi, accepted the younger foreign Moabite, Ruth, as truly a family member, while Ruth refused to desert Naomi and loved her. Two women, of differing generations and differing nations, banded together. Two childless widows, trapped within the patriarchal Mosaic Law, managed to utilize the Law to their own advantage.

The village elders called upon YHWH to bless Ruth, to make her "Like Rachel and Leah who together built up the House of Israel."[9] They compare Ruth to the Matriarch although she is a woman of Moab. But, like Sarah, Ruth left her homeland, her people, her idols to follow the way of YHWH.

In Matthew's genealogy of Jesus, Ruth joins Rahab and Bathsheba as alien women who are ancestors of Christ.

Hannah

Do Not Take Me for a Worthless Woman

I Sam 1:16

It was near the end of the harvest season, a time of joy and gratitude for the fertility of the land, the generosity of YHWH.

Elkanah, with his two wives, Hannah and Peninnah, traveled to Shiloh to celebrate the Feast of Tabernacles and to share the portions of the sacrificial meal. Peninnah, who had children, taunted Hannah because she was barren. Although Hannah was the more beloved wife, like Sarah, Rebekah and Rachel, she yearned for a son. Every year when the family traveled to Shiloh to keep the Feast of Tabernacles, Hannah, dejected and weeping, could not eat of the sacrificial meal. Distribution of the sacrificial portions only accentuated Hannah's infertility. At every meal, Peninnah reminded Hannah that YHWH had made her barren.[1]

After one such meal, Hannah, from the depths of her grief, implored YHWH for a son. She bargained with YHWH, pledging the child to the service of YHWH for his entire life. She desired a child so desperately that she was willing to forego the joys of mothering and give him away after weaning. Hannah prayed for a long time, her lips moving without any sound. Eli, the High Priest of the Temple of YHWH, sat on his impressive seat near the doorpost of the Temple.

Eli, who had been watching her, assumed that she was drunk and scolded, "Rid yourself of your wine."[2] Hannah, however, responded without fear and with dignity. Gently she chided the High Priest. "Do not take me for a worthless woman," she said and explained that she had taken no wine or strong drink. She then proceeded to tell Eli that she had been speaking with YHWH. Eli then blessed her and she felt dejected no longer. Within the year, barren Hannah had conceived and borne a son whom she called Samuel. When Samuel was weaned, about three years of age, Hannah brought him to the Temple and left him there to serve YHWH.

It was at this point that Hannah uttered her Canticle of Praise and Thanksgiving to YHWH. Hannah's Canticle foreshadowed the Canticle of Mary of Nazareth, called the Magnificat. Both canticles demonstrate knowledge and appreciation of the omnipotence and mercy of YHWH. Hannah also foreshadowed Elizabeth, mother of John the Baptizer. Like Elizabeth, Hannah was presumed to be barren. Hannah's son, Samuel, a prophet and judge, anointed Saul, the first king of Israel. Elizabeth's son, John, anointed (baptized) Jesus, the Christ, called the King of Peace.

Hannah, Elkanah, Peninnah returned to the Temple and visited Samuel annually. Eventually, YHWH sent Hannah an additional three sons and two daughters.

Hannah, like Sarah, Rebekah, Rachel, was labelled 'barren'. Like Sarah, Rebekah and Rachel, Hannah spoke with YHWH Who intervened on her behalf. Her faith in YHWH, like that of the Matriarchs, fostered the fulfillment of God's Covenantal promise.

Israelite Kings

Solomon Became a Follower of Astarte, the Goddess

I Kings 11:5

Samuel, son of Hannah, grew up and YHWH was with him. Now as Samuel aged, he was known from the far north near Phoenicia to

34

the Negeb in the south as a stalwart prophet of YHWH. He was judge over Israel so long as he lived. But the Israelites, consistently wayward, rejected YHWH's kingship and the leadership of Israelite judges. In their desire to become like other tribes they wanted a human king. Even though Samuel warned them against such an innovation, the Israelites refused to listen.

A stalwart Benjaminite called Saul, in the prime of his life, had been wandering for weeks searching for his father's lost livestock. His food supply was exhausted and he was lost. Then he met 'some girls'[1] who directed him to Samuel. Samuel anointed Saul who was tall, head and shoulders above the people. He was also the handsomest man in Israel. Such was the beauty of the first Israelite king.[2] Saul began his reign by counselling the Israelites to follow YHWH.[3] But Saul offended YHWH very early in his reign. Then Samuel informed Saul that the Lord would remove his kingship and give it to another. Throughout his years as king, there were fierce wars and every strong man of Israel was recruited into Saul's army. YWHW's spirit left Saul and a young man of Bethlehem, great-grandson of Ruth, entered Saul's service, slew Goliath, became his son-in-law. Eventually, Saul, king of the Israelites, resented his son-in-law, David, whose military victories made him the favorite hero and it was apparent to Saul that YHWH was with David. So Saul planned David's death. But David's wife, Michal, daughter of King Saul, warned David, helped him to escape and saved his life. When David was fleeing Saul, another woman, Abigail, wife of Nabal, also saved David's life. After Nabal's death David married Abigail. Micah and Abigail, together with the unnamed girls of Saul's experience, preserved the Israelite kings, hence YHWH's Covenant, by timely intervention.

The mantle of Covenant settled on David, son of Jesse of Bethleham, ancestor of Jesus.[4] YHWH spoke again, "I will preserve the offspring of your body after you and make his sovereignty secure and your throne established forever."[5] David became king and under his rule the Israelite tribes finally coalesced into a powerful empire. A musician, statesman, poet, David was also a brave and cunning warrior, who won victories over the Philistines, Moabites, Arameans, Edomites. During his reign, as Egypt's power faded, its wealth was usurped by the priestly class.[6] Although David recaptured Jerusalem,

35

revered the Ark of God, offered holocausts to YHWH, he sinned by seducing Bathsheba, and by arranging for the death of her husband, Uriah. He coveted Bathsheba and wed her after Uriah died. David further offended YHWH by initiating a census of the Israelites. In Israel, the people belonged to God rather than to the king and it was believed that none other than YHWH should know their number.

As David neared death, Adonijah, son of Haggith, another wife of David, plotted for the kingdom against Solomon, David's son by Bathsheba. But Bathsheba implored David to act upon his promise that their son, Solomon, would succeed him to the throne. In response to her plea, David instructed the priest, Zadok, to anoint Solomon immediately. Bathsheba, like many female predecessors, preserved the Covenant. Under King Solomon it appeared that the Covenant of YHWH was fulfilled. The original Covenant with Sarah and Abraham promised a multitude of nations, issue of kings, the whole of land of Canaan and "I will be your God."[7]

Under King David the Israelites had expanded their territory and become a mighty nation, subjecting many other tribes. Solomon's realm extended from the mountains of Lebanon in the northwest to the Red Sea in the south. Under King Solomon, Phoenicians, Tyrenians, Thebans worked along with the Israelites, forming a multitude of peoples. All the important caravan routes traversed Solomon's land. Such trade routes enriched his kingdom monetarily, philosophically, artistically, culturally. Solomon's wealth was phenomenal. He maintained a large standing army of forty thousand horses and twelve thousand horsemen plus archers and charioteers. Solomon built himself a luxurious palace of cedar, dressed stone and bronze. He used only golden drinking vessels. His courtiers, both female and male, wore golden jewelry set with exquisite gems. In his court people were dressed in colorful garments, since weaving and dyeing were practiced in his realm with great skill. Music was an integral part of daily life. Singers, dancers, harpists entertained everywhere. Solomon imported ebony, sandalwood, gold, silver, ivory as well as exotic animals such as peacocks and apes. The glory of YHWH filled the great Temple built at Solomon's direction. Solomon, the third great king of Israel, was indeed the wisest and the wealthiest king.

But Solomon's wisdom was not holiness. Solomon failed to fulfill the Covenant. In contempt for Mosaic Law, Solomon married Pharaoh's daughter, as well as Moabite, Edomite, Sidonian and Hittite women. He retained many concubines. Neither his many wives nor his concubines revered YHWH. So Solomon built ziggurats to the other gods where his women burned incense and sacrificed to alien gods. Solomon adored Astarte, Chemosh, Milcom. Solomon, upon whom YHWH had poured love, wisdom, power and wealth, turned away from the God of Sarah, Hagar, Rebekah, Leah, Rachel, Jochebed, Miriam, Rahab, Deborah and Hannah. Solomon had reigned over all of Israel for forty years. However, in less than forty years following his death, Solomon's kingdom split into two segments: Israel and Judah. Israel, called the Northern Kingdom, comprised ten of the Israelite tribes: descendants of Reuben, Simeon, Zebulun, Isaachar, Dan, Gad, Asher, Naphtali, Ephraim and Manasseh. The remaining two tribes, descendants of Judah and Benjamin plus a portion of the priestly tribe of Levi were called the kingdom of Judah.

The Northern Kingdom, after the conquest in 722 B.C. was dispersed and became known as the lost tribes. Scholars theorize concerning the location of their descendants throughout Arabia, India, the Americas, Europe and Africa. But their true fate remains unknown.

Huldah

Go and Consult YHWH on Behalf of Me

2 Kings 22:12

Following the death of Solomon and the schism which separated Israel from Judah, the House of David suffered from many wars and unjust kings who perpetuated adoration of idols. Of the many kings who ruled Israel, Hezekiah remained most faithful to YHWH. He abolished the ziggurats, the sacred poles, and smashed the bronzed idols of pagan gods, some of which were in the Temple of YHWH. Following Hezekiah's death, two wicked kings, both of whom defiled the Temple, ruled in utter contempt of YHWH. Around 650 B.C., Josiah came to the throne, at the age of eight years. In the eighteenth year of his reign, he arranged for repairs to be made to the Temple. During the course of this project, the High Priest, Kilkiah, found the Book of the Sacred Law, which had been lost during the reign of Manasseh, father of the previous king.[1] Scholars disagree on the origin of the book. Was it in fact the Mosaic Law or was it a manuscript from Hezekiah? However, the Book was read aloud to King Josiah, who was appalled to learn that the precepts outlined within the text had not been followed. The king gave orders to his priest, scribe and minister. "Go and consult with YHWH, on behalf of me and the people, about the contents of the Book which has been found."[2] The High Priest, scribe, and the minister went to the Second Quarter of Jerusalem, to Huldah, the prophet. She was the wife of Shallum, but evidently that was not her major role. Apparently she was the recognized voice of YHWH in her community, known to the priest, the scribe and the minister. Huldah said, "YHWH, the God Of Israel, says this…" Huldah then explained that YHWH had predicted disaster for the kingdom because the Israelites had deserted YHWH, except for Josiah, whose heart had followed the Lord. Because of Josiah's faithfulness, he would be spared and would be gathered to his ancestors in peace before any of the predicted disasters occurred.

Following her pronouncements, serious religious reform was initiated. Josiah ordered the removal of all cult objects which were burned outside the walls of Jerusalem. He eliminated the spurious priests who had sacrificed to Baal, to the sun, the moon and the zodiac, destroyed the apartments of the 'sacred prostitutes.' He razed all pagan altars and temples and expelled necromancers and wizards. Scripture says of him, "No king before him had turned to YHWH as he did, with all his heart."[3] Huldah motivated Josiah's extensive religious reform and foretold YHWH's mercy to him. Despite Josiah's reforms, the tribes frequently engaged in inter-tribal war, struggled against the Arameans and the Assyrians. King followed king and with rare exception offended YHWH, fostering abominable practices during the years of their reigns. Most of the Israelites were again mired in idolatry. They built ziggurats, erected sacred poles to honor idols and practiced divination and sorcery.

Generally, the kings of the tribes of the Kingdom of Judah did not desist from offending YHWH. During many years the people of Judah continued to burn incense and offer sacrifice to pagan gods. Despite repeated warnings from prophets, the princes of Judah added sin to sin, practicing idolatry, polluting the Temple of the Lord by indulging in human sacrifice, immolating their own sons. Such practice was repugnant to YHWH. Eventually, the Chaldeans invaded Jerusalem, destroyed most of the people of the tribe of Judah. The survivors were brought in shame and captivity to Babylon.

So, despite the courage and tenacity of many Israelite women, named and unnamed, the Covenant seemed lost. Abrogated by male leaders of Israel, the glory was gone, the battles lost, the Temple destroyed. Huldah's prophecy was fulfilled.

In the opinion of one scholar, "At the beginning of the crucial judgment about which books are to be accepted as Canon of the Bible (authentic), we find a woman."[4] Rome teaches that it was through the Apostolic Tradition that the Church knew which books were to be included in the list of Sacred Books. The Canon of Scripture was defined for Roman Catholics at the Council of Trent, in the sixteenth century[5] but long before the Apostles existed, Huldah, a woman, certified the Book of Law as Canon of Scripture. During the centuries-long process of Canonical validation, within Judaism and Christianity, Huldah was the original certifier.[6]

The Canon of Scripture is the rock upon which Tradition and much of Magisterium rest. Scripture, Tradition, Magisterium, the elements cited by Rome as refusing sacerdotal ordination to women, are all profoundly influenced by a woman.

YHWH

The Lord Is a God of Justice Who Knows No Favorites
                                                    Sirach 35:12-14

While the glaciers retreated towards the polar regions, mastodons, woolly mammoths, saber-toothed carnivores, oversized wolves competed with humans for sustenance. For uncounted centuries, long before any oral tradition developed, small groups of humans, loosely affiliated by blood, gathered and consumed vegetables, roots, fruits, nuts. Some of the more enterprising persons among them hunted small animals or harvested food from the lakes, rivers, seas. Unclothed, unskilled, without any reliable shelters, our forebears struggled to survive. Their lives were dominated by the ebb and flow of food as dictated by the tides, the rains, or the seasons of the sun. Unable to have any significant impact upon their environment, our ancestors were at the mercy of forces beyond their control...with one significant exception: the female could produce new life. In early antiquity, pre-historic humans believed that all females could conceive, bear and deliver offspring without any male participation.

Earliest examples of goddesses depict females without heads: all breasts, protuberant bellies, vulvae.[1] Such icons demonstrate the power that primitive tribes attributed to female-ness and reproduction. Eve expressed this belief when she said, "I have acquired a man with the help of YHWH."[2] Mythological remains of such belief systems are still evident in parthenogenesis of certain Mediterranean goddesses such as Gaia.[3] From about 25,000 B.C. to approximately 8,000 B.C., no evidence of a male deity exists.[4] Females were considered to be the source of life and the Earth was perceived to be the source of the elements which support life: food, water, shelter and security. Such assumptions were evident in the belief systems of the people. From circa 8,000 B.C. to 2,500 B.C., worship of the Great Goddess, the Earth Mother, existed throughout the Indus Valley, the Near East, the Balkans, Asia, Egypt and Eastern Mediterreanean Lands.[5] She was worshipped under many names, ie, Mengai, Ixchel,

An, Ambika, Marigamma. The Babylonians and Assyrians worshipped Ishtar as an omnipotent mother goddess while the Sumerians believed that the Creator lived within the womb of the Great Earth Mother, sometimes called Inanna. This belief is similar to the ancient Chinese belief that all creation had emerged from a cosmic womb and all would return thence. The Japanese adored Amatersau, the Great Goddess who presided over life, health, fertility, order and cleanliness.[6]

As animal husbandry grew, with its concomitant awareness of the male contribution to reproduction, deities were allowed to be male. Such early gods were the stag, bear, wolf, alligator, eagle. They personified the strength, speed, courage and cunning of the herds of wild antelope, bison, deer, caribou upon which the hunters depended for food, clothing, shelter. Eventually, deities were perceived to be of either gender. Peoples who depended upon rivers or seas for food or commerce, perceived the waters to be animated with gods and goddesses. They were called Ler, Van, Neptune, Proteus, Nina. Agrarian tribes, in addition to the Earth Goddess, developed veneration for the sun, called Lugh, Sol, Ra, Dius, Helios. Usually, the sun deity was believed to be male while the earth goddess continued as female. Eventually, the goddess and the god were believed to be lovers. Ishtar and Tammuz of Babylonia and Assyria, or Isis and Osiris of Egypt are examples.

Perhaps the most powerful of the celestial deities was the moon goddess called Thoth, Nana, Sin, Selene, Diana, Luna. Lunar symbolism helped humanity to appreciate the concept of 'cycle'. Lunar cycles governed the tides, crops, and female fecundity. The cycles of life include becoming, growing, maturing, waning, dying and becoming again. Each of these cycles was represented in the recurring phases of the moon. The major feasts of the world's monotheistic religions, including Christianity and Judaism, are still scheduled in relation to the phases of the moon.

In most cultures, hosts of lesser gods and goddesses were believed to preside over every function of life. Each town, village and dwelling place had its own particular deity. Eventually many polytheistic religions evolved into a belief in a Supreme God. In Africa, Onyame and Kwoth were venerated as superior to a host of lesser gods, while the Mayans of Yucatan adored Humab Ku as a superior God who reigned over many lesser gods.[7]

The concept of a Creator-Sustainer developed in response to fundamental needs.[8] From the Great Spirits of indigenous tribes, through manifestations surrounding the sun, moon, wind and the seas, through the constructed idols of many societies, to the awareness of the ONE-WHO-IS, God has been refracted through the prism of all cultures. For many, YHWH is the culmination of eons of theological evolution. YWHW is the Uncaused Cause whose love and power endures forever. YHWH changes deserts into streams of living water. YHWH's love is better than life. YHWH is one of the names of the God of monotheism. Yet, who is YHWH?

> Bear yourself blameless in my presence…I will be your God[9]
> I am YHWH, your God who brought you out of the land of
> Egypt, out of the house of slavery[10]
> I Am Who Am[11]
> I, I am YHWH, there is no other savior but me[12]

YHWH expressed the Divine Presence through many symbols, i.e., a smoking furnace, a firebrand,[13] the burning bush,[14] a cloud, fire, trumpet blasts, thunder, lightning flashes.[15]

Terah, the father of Sarah and Abraham, served other gods.[16] But, Sarah and Abraham were called from such practice. They, with all their posterity, were called to worship YHWH. For Sarah and Abraham, YHWH was "God Most High, Creator of Heaven and Earth."[17] The Qu'ran, Islam's Holy Scripture, describes Abraham smashing idols into fragments [18] and praying to God Most High to turn his sons away from serving idols. Sarah converted women to the service of YHWH. It is this intuitive recognition of and fidelity to the One-Who-Is that represent Sarah's and Abraham's greatest gift to history.

Judaism, Christianity and Islam all revere Abraham as the father of their faith. But, Sarah and Hagar are ignored, victims of centuries of male prejudice. Patriarchy perceived YHWH as an all powerful, judgmental warrior-god who was lauded for Israel's military victories, power and wealth. Perceiving God as specifically male legitimized the subjection of women. However, Scripture, despite evident patriarchal influence, frequently expressed YHWH as female. YHWH says:

> I groan like a woman in labor [19]
> I have carried you since you were born [20]
> Like a son comforted by his mother, so will I comfort you [21]
>
> She is the breath and power of God [22]
> I stooped to feed my child [23]

Chapter ten of the Book of Wisdom extols the feminine aspect of YHWH from Adam to Moses. Adam, the first man, had Her for his protector. She, Wisdom, piloted Noah on a paltry piece of wood. She saved Lot from fire and brimstone. She delivered Jacob from the anger of his brother, Esau. She did not forsake Joseph when he was sold, but kept him free from pain. She entered the soul of Moses and delivered a holy people from a nation of oppressors. She, Wisdom, opened the mouths of the dumb and gave speech to the tongues of babes. She, Wisdom, is shelter by day and starlight through the night.

But, to try to assign gender to the Alive, Ever-Real-Reality, the ALWAYS-AM is the undertaking of a fool.

After the division of Israel and during its political decline, Isaiah emerged as one of Israel's most significant prophets. He evoked an image of the Messiah: "a maiden is with child." Instead of the safely-clean-barren-postmenopausal woman, the image of a young pregnant virgin was presented. Isaiah called this child Emmanuel, which means "God Is With Us."

Humanity's perception of the Creator-Sustainer had evolved yet again.

NEW TESTAMENT

Jesus' Mandate

Of the one hundred sixty-six Christian denominations in the United States which responded to a recent poll, eighty-four ordain females, eighty-two do not. Obviously, there is no clear-cut direction in such data. For many, the question remains unanswered. Theologians, Biblical scholars, feminists, misogynists have researched, debated and written about the issue of ordination of females. And now, John Paul II tells Roman Catholics to stop all discussions. But the questions remain:

What did Jesus really want?
What is an Apostle? Do women fulfill the role?
What is a priest? Do women fulfill the role?

The status of women rose and fell throughout recorded history. According to Swidler[1] periods of high status in Egypt were 3,000 to 2270 B.C., 1580 to 1085 B.C. and 663 B.C. to 375 A.D.; in Greece 3,000 B.C. to 1,000 B.C. then deteriorating until 450 B.C. Despite such fluctuations in women's status, certain aspects of the feminine remained almost universally suspect, i.e., menstruation. Superstitious fear of and aversion to a menstruous woman, and sometimes a pregnant woman, were transcultural. Menstrual blood was credited with very powerful and harmful magic. Such blood was believed to be capable of killing crops, blighting flowers, souring wine. Zoroastrians believed that women, who were deemed unclean, were under the influence of demons during their menses, pregnancy and childbirth. The Hindus believed the pregnant woman was impure, while the Buddhists banned menstruating women from their temples. The Romans believed menstrual blood could cause madness in dogs, while the Jews believed a menstruating woman was ritually unclean. The Law of Leviticus deemed a woman to be unclean for forty days following the birth of a son, but she was unclean for eighty days after a daughter's birth. As in other cultures, Jewish women were forbidden entry to the Woman's Court of the Temple during their times of uncleanness. In many cultures, the state of being unclean was usually suspended prior to menarche and after menopause. Apparently, when women were unable to participate in the mysterious power-filled ability to bring forth new life, they were not threatening, hence not unclean.

Jesus, the human person, lived in Palestine, a land occupied by the Roman army. Tiberius (42 B.C.-37 A.D.) sat as Emperor in Rome while Herod Antipas served as tetrarch of Galilee and Peraea. The Jewish natives resented the occupational forces while the Romans held the Jews in contempt. And both the Romans and the Jews disdained women. They were not unusual in this regard. Like females in other cultures, women occupied nebulous roles among the Jews of Jesus' time. They usually existed only in relationship to men: a daughter, sister, wife, mother, mother-in-law, widow, harlot. And during the ministry of Jesus, one can see Him interacting with woman in each role: daughter (of Jairus), sister(of Lazarus), wife (of Chuza), mother (of Jesus), mother-in-law (of Peter), widow (of Nain), harlot (woman accused of adultery).

A multitude of words have addressed the fact that Jesus consorted with outcasts. Repetition, coupled with some degree of boredom, has dulled the reality. But, in Jesus' culture, women were socially inferior, non-entities. They were considered to be impotent persons whose testimony was not accepted in court. Usually, they were without inheritance rights. Yet, Jesus cured women, ate with them, forgave them, accepted their support and ministry to Him. Actually, He commissioned them to speak in His name.

Throughout Israel's history, YHWH stooped to humanity's ways, utilizing humanity's symbols, to communicate with the people. YHWH sent Melchizidech to Abraham to accept his tithes and to bless him. With Abraham, YHWH used sacrificial animals and burning firebrands on Moriah. With Moses, God used fire on Sinai. YHWH manifested the Self through fire, thunder, lightning. These symbols were gender-free. Then Jesus, YHWH's Word, stooped to humanity's condition. As God, Jesus could have manifested the Self in any one of many ways. Jesus could have walked into town, like

Melchizedech, without any prior history, or, like the manifestation to Sarah and Abraham at Mamre.[2] Jesus could have appeared upon a mountaintop in a burning bush. But Jesus was known to be of human estate. Jesus was born of woman.[3] And in selecting to be born of woman, Jesus immediately and forever consecrated the basic physiology of the female. Immediately and forever, menstrual and childbirth bloods were embraced; a rebuke to the males of pagan nations and the Law of Leviticus.[4]

Jesus, in the New Covenant, selected unclean symbols: childbirth, water and blood. From His birth through His death to the Eucharist today, Jesus uses the ancient symbols: water and blood. But these symbols -water and blood - are gender-specific: they are uniquely female.

This is evident initially in the details involved in Jesus' birth. Matthew (1:25) and Luke (2:6-7) both tell how Mary gave birth to a son. Jesus, believed by Christians to be God, passed through the birth canal and emerged slimy with amniotic water and blood, ritually unclean. Jesus was not born of a post-menopausal woman, one who was safely 'clean'. Jesus was birthed of a young woman. The Omnipotent, Omniscient, Creator-Sustainer, the Ancient-One-Who-Does-Not-Change, the Always-AM, divested the Self of all power and entered the world through a ritually unclean female. By using feminine symbols, Jesus raised females from their subservience. He wanted to raise all, both female and male, to equality before God, to render religion free from gender bias. "What God has made clean, you have no right to call profane."[5]

One can trace Jesus' use of water and blood plus the use of birth and rebirth to focus upon the dignity, freedom, equality and apostleship of women. Matthew (3:13-17), Mark (1:9-11), Luke (3:21-23) and John (1:29-34) all recount the baptism of Jesus in the Jordan River. Jesus initiated His public ministry by immersing Himself in water, the chief component of amniotic fluid.[6]

According to the Synoptic Gospels, Jesus was led by the Spirit into the wilderness, fasting for forty days. And in the spare language of Scripture, He was hungry...very hungry. Then the tempter devil, Satan, challenged Jesus, "If you are the Son of God," turn these stones into bread. Jesus refused, quoting Deuteronomy, "Man does not live by bread alone." Some of the Church fathers interpreted this temptation to be 'of the flesh', in other words, sexual, anti-female. However, Jesus fasted forty days recalling the forty years which the Israelites spent wandering through the wilderness. The lesson from Jesus' quotation in Deuteronomy[7] is to follow YHWH and reverence YHWH. The interaction between Jesus and Satan was a temptation concerning the truth of Jesus' identity, "If you are the Son of God." Jesus was tempted towards power when Satan offered Him the splendor and glory of all the kingdoms of the world. Jesus was tempted away from YHWH when Satan asked Him to throw himself off the Temple parapet.

Note here the absence of the woman as temptress, the absence of woman as evil. Untruth, unbelief, power are the trials, not Eve, nor woman, nor sex.

At Cana, Jesus performed His first miracle. John (2:1-12) tells of the marriage feast, the request of Mary, Jesus' mother, a woman. The guests had exhausted the supply of wine, so Jesus changed water into wine. So, the first of Jesus' miracles used the feminine symbol of Eucharist: water and wine, wine being representative of blood.

Soon after this event, Jesus was in Jerusalem for Passover. One of the pharisees, Nicodemus, a leader among the people, came to see Jesus, during the night. For a pharisee, learned in the Law, prominent among the people, meeting with an itinerant preacher would have seemed questionable at best, hence the night visit.

Pharisees insisted upon strict observance of Jewish Law, and were extremely conscientious concerning its fine points. As a Pharisee, Nicodemus would have been acutely aware of the ritual uncleanness of birth. Yet Jesus used the symbol of birth (blood and water) in His discourse with Nicodemus. Jesus spoke of rebirth through water and the Spirit, explained by many theologians to be symbolic of baptism. In this interaction, Jesus, male, spoke to Nicodemus, male, about a rebirth, a Christian sacrament, Baptism. Yet, the Roman Catholic Church does not limit baptism to males. The only Christian Sacrament limited by Rome to males is Holy Orders (ordination to priesthood). Why?

Jesus left Judea, heading for Galilee, through Samaria. Samaritans believed that Mount Gerazim, in Samaria, was the proper site for sacrificial prayer to YHWH. Since the Samaritans rejected Jerusalem as the site for prayer, they were considered to be heretics hence outcasts.

Once again, John is raconteur. In chapter four, he describes the scene. About noon, Jesus, tired, hungry and thirsty sat beside Jacob's Well (Bir Ya'cob). This event recalls the similarity between the Samaritan woman and the stories of Rebekah, Rachel and Zipporah, each of whom had been encountered beside a well. Each had been essential to the Covenant. Now another woman is encountered beside a well, symbolic of the continuity of the female role in YHWH's Covenant.

The disciples had gone into the town to buy food, and Jesus was waiting for them to return. A Samaritan woman came to draw water. Jesus said to her, "Give me a drink." The unnamed woman replied, "How is it that you, a Jew, ask a drink of me, a woman of Samaria?"

Her question is threefold: "You, a Jew." Jews did not associate with Samaritans.[8]

"Me, a woman." It was breaking the Law to speak with a woman who was not of one's tribe, especially a Samaritan, who was believed to be ritually unclean.

"Of Samaria." Samaritans were heretics, outcasts.

Her question to Jesus demonstrates a woman of intelligence, who is aware of Jewish Law and, perhaps is resentful of the hypocrisy of the customs of her day. She shows neither fear nor submission in her response to the Jewish stranger. When Jesus answers, "If you knew the gift of God, and who it is that is asking you, 'Give me a drink', you would have asked him and he would have given you living water." Now her attitude softens and she calls Jesus, "Sir". She notes that He has no implement for carrying water and asks, "Are you greater than our father, Jacob?" Now the conversation has become theological in nature. She realizes that Jesus is in fact greater than Jacob and asks "Sir, give me this water." But Jesus replies, "Go, call your husband, and come here." She answers, "I have no husband." Although she has lived with six men, she has had no spouse. Jesus says, "You spoke truly." The Samaritan woman replies, "Sir, I see you are a prophet."

Then they converse concerning the true place of worship and she introduces the subject of the Messiah. Jesus reveals that He is the Messiah. Jesus, for the first recorded time, identifies Himself as Messiah. Jesus selects a woman from an alien tribe, who has a questionable history, as the first human to learn of His Divinity. She immediately left her water jar and went into the city and spoke to the people there saying, "Come." The people followed her out of the city to find Jesus.

Jesus commissioned the Samaritan woman when He said, "Go, call...and come here." Jesus shared His mission with her when He said, "I am He."

Many Samaritans there believed in Him because of her testimony[9] and at their request, He stayed in that place for two days.

Jesus selected a female, an outcast, to bring the Good News to an entire community. Jesus told His disciples, "Lift up your eyes and see how the fields are ripe for harvest. I sent you to reap that for which you did not labor." The Samaritan woman had trudged back to the city in the heat of the day, spoken to the people who were now coming out of the city to meet Jesus. The Samaritan woman had labored, had sown the seeds of faith. Now, His disciples might reap.

The Samaritan woman was an apostle since Jesus called her and sent her. She spoke the Good News and brought followers to Jesus. Jesus, in His interaction with the Samaritan woman used the female symbol, water and blood. The Well of Jacob is the water. The ritually unclean Samaritan female is the 'menstruous woman'. As such she represents blood. And Jesus, again as in His discourse with Nicodemus, lifted all - female and male - above gender when He said, "God is spirit and those who worship must worship in spirit[10] and truth." Spirit knows no gender.

Matthew (9:18-26), Mark (5:21-43) and Luke (8:40-56) all tell of the daughter of Jairus and the woman with a hemorrhage. Mark recounts Jesus' crossing of the water in a boat and staying by the lakeside. Then while Jairus pleaded for his daughter's cure, a woman who had been bleeding for twelve years touched his cloak and was cured. The woman (unnamed, like the Samaritan woman) after long and painful treatment had spent all she had, and she was getting worse. Leviticus (15:19-33) is quite specific in her situation: she was unclean. Anyone who touched her also became unclean. Any bed, seat, dishes, food, clothing, in fact, anything that she had touched, was also unclean. For twelve years, she had been unclean. Her life had been circumscribed by pain, fear, isolation and the ostracism of uncleanness. In her desperation (and faith) she broke the Law and touched the hem of Jesus' cloak. All three Gospel writers say that Jesus called her "My daughter" a term of endearment, of security. Note here that Jesus was not troubled by any legal notion of uncleanness, nor by the proscriptions of the Law. He praises her for her faith, told her to go "in peace and be freed of your complaint."

Here again, Jesus used the feminine symbol: water and blood. The lake represents the water, the hemorrhage represents blood.

Jairus was a 'ruler of the synogogue', a man of some social stature in the community. He was not unclean, not ostracised, not an outcast like the woman with the hemorrhage. Jairus pleaded with Jesus to cure his daughter. Jesus excluded all from the room of the little girl, except Peter, James, John and the parents of the little girl. Here, Jesus included the mother. According to custom, she would not have been expected to be present. But Jesus included her, granting her respect and dignity. The daughter of Jairus was twelve years old. Some have likened her age to the number of the tribes of Israel, but her age is that normally concerned with menarche. She is old enough to begin to menstruate, to become ritually unclean. Again, the feminine symbol: water (the tears of the mourners) and blood (her age, twelve years). This little girl had been declared dead, therefore unclean. Jesus, in apparent breach of the Law, touched her, restored her life and instructed the members of her community to give her something to eat. Give her bread. Give her the living bread. Give her Eucharist. Allow her access to ordained ministry of the Eucharist.

Jesus carried the feminine symbol to the Last Supper. Matthew, Mark and Luke all recall the institution of the Eucharist, specifically, "This is my blood." Jesus, at the Last Supper used the feminine symbol: water and blood.

John tells that Jesus always loved those who were His, but now He showed how perfect that love was. Jesus got up from the table, wrapped a towel around His waist, poured water into a basin and began to wash the disciples' feet. Jesus had not reverted to the ritual ablutions of the Law, like the Pharisees. He was using water to complete the feminine symbol. Also, Jesus, by washing the feet, taught a supremely important lesson: that of service, translated from Greek diakonos, root word for deacon. Jewish females were expected to wash the feet and the hair of their husbands, so in washing the feet of His disciples, Jesus was also uniting the tasks of females with the tasks of His priesthood.

John, in his account of the Eucharistic discourse of Jesus, which comprises chapters fourteen, fifteen and sixteen, remembers Jesus' reference to a woman in childbirth, the unclean symbol. Luke tells of Jesus' anguish as he prayed in Gethsemane, the 'bloody sweat'[11] "his sweat fell to the ground like great drops of blood."[12]

During the Jewish Feast of Tabernacles, Jesus taught in the Temple of Jerusalem.[13] And on the final day of the Festival, Jesus cried aloud, "If anyone is thirsty, come to me!" John follows this quotation with the comment, "As Scripture says: from His breast shall flow fountains of living water." This quotation is an apt reference to the blood and water flowing from Jesus' breast after the Roman soldier pierced it with a lance.

Jesus also said, "I tell you most solemnly, whoever welcomes the one I send, welcomes me." Well, Jesus sent females. He sent the Samaritan woman and the women on Easter morning who were commissioned to tell the message of His resurrection. Hence, the ban on female ordination is in direct conflict with Jesus' mandate. Jesus, from His birth, throughout His ministry, at His death used the ancient feminine symbol of birth: water and blood. He selected this symbol to free woman from subservience, to make her forever ritually clean, to relate her in a specific way to the Eucharist.

Mary of Magdala

You Are a Priest Forever, According to the Order of Melchizedek
Hebrew 7:18

Who was Mary of Magdala? Was she Isis, the pagan goddess or was she the Evangelist of Gaul? Was she the Black Madonna or the Primary Apostle of the Risen Christ? Why have artists portrayed her as a repentant whore?

Some writers allege that devotion to Mary of Magdala is merely a Christianized version of belief in Isis. Isis (Egypt), like Aphrodite (Greece), Venus (Rome), and Freyja (Norselands), was adored as the omnipotent earth-mother-goddess of love, beauty, fertility. Like Freyja, Isis possessed great magic and was a sorceress. In ancient Germanic myth, Andhumla, a primeval cow, emerged from the original abyss and nourished the first living creature, Ymir.[1] A similarity exists in Egyptian mythology, in that the consort-god of Isis, called Osiris, inhabited the body of a sacred bull, Apis. In some ancient Egyptian art, Isis, too, is portrayed as a bovine creature. Later, however, under Hellenistic influence, Isis was idealized into a beautiful woman with ringlets framing a serene face. Veneration of the Hellenized Isis spread from Egypt throughout the lands surrounding the Mediterranean Sea. Her cult was particularly popular in the area of southwestern Europe known variably as Gaul, Provincia, Provence, southeast France. The principal centers for urban living in the area were Marseilles, Arles, Cannes, Avignon, Nice. These cities continue to be important entities in SE France. In each of these centers the people adored Isis and remains of her temples still exist. Coincidentally, devotion to Mary of Magdala flourishes in these areas. There is a very old legend that describes a journey of Mary of Magdala, Martha and Lazarus of Bethany, Mary Jacobi, Mary Salome, Joseph of Arimethea and others across the Mediterranean Sea from the Holy Land to Gaul. They debarked in an area now called the south of France near the village known as Saintes Maries de la Mer (Saints Marys of the Sea). It was a land of exquisite beauty, bordered by the waters of the Mediterranean Sea on the southeast. Olive trees, flowering shrubs, grapes flourished in this land, later memorialized by Van Gogh and Gauguin. And here, local folk lore says, Mary of Magdala planted the seeds of Christianity. She evangelized throughout the area, especially in Marseilles, preaching on the steps of a Temple of Diana.[2] Throughout the region are many shrines, chapels, churches dedicated to Mary of Magdala. Villages and streets are named for her, a tribute to her role as evangelist. July 22 is her feast day, and annually on this day, her devotees produce parades, concerts, fairs, novenas and liturgies in her honor. Several sites boast possession of relics purported to be her skeletal parts. Such faithful behavior has continued unabated for centuries. But another devotion co-exists in SE France: the cult of the Black Madonna. Strangely enough, the icons of the Black Madonnas appear to be concentrated within the centers of devotion to Mary of Magdala. According to some writers[3] fifty shrines of Mary of Magdala also contain icons of the Black Madonna, sometimes revered as the Black Virgin. The icons present the typical images of a mother and child. Most of the icons appear to have Eastern or Byzantine influence. What is unique, however, is the fact that the mother and child are black-skinned. Although explanations for the black skin are extant[4] some authors[5] claim a paganistic (Isis) link between the Black Madonnas and a further link with Mary of Magdala.

In central Ethiopia there was a village called 'Magdala' and in northeastern Egypt there was a town called 'Magdalum.'[6] If in fact Mary of Magdala originated in either of these places, one might postulate that Mary of Magdala was dark or black skinned. However, the Black Madonna or the Black Virgin icons portray a mother and child. There is no evidence that Mary of Magdala ever bore a child, hence the allegation that Mary of Magdala is the Black Madonna is most likely erroneous. Furthermore, there are many other shrines to the Black Madonna in Europe, Asia, the Americas in absence of any particular devotion to Mary of Magdala.

In addition to the sites in Ethiopia and Egypt, there was another village, a prosperous hamlet on the northwest shore of the Sea of Galilee, called 'elMejdel'. Mary of Magdala most likely came from there. Having come from a 'prosperous' village would correspond with her Scriptural persona. Chronologically, within Scripture, Luke is the first to speak about Mary of Magdala when he describes her as one of those who took care of Jesus. Luke describes Jesus traveling through towns and villages preaching, healing. The Twelve went with Him along with Mary of Magdala, Joanna the wife of Chuza, Susanna and others who 'provided for them out of their own resources.' Apparently, Mary was independent and wealthy enough to contribute significant financial aid. With one exception[7] in every Biblical reference where Mary and several others are cited, Mary is listed first, an indication of primacy in Scripture. Other than primacy among female disciples of Jesus, what does Scripture say about Mary of Magdala?

Most scholars agree that Mark is the earliest version and the cornerstone of the Synoptic Gospels. Mark does not mention Mary of Magdala by name until nearly the end of his Gospel where he notes that while Jesus hung dying on the cross, "there were some women watching from a distance. Among them were Mary of Magdala, Mary who was the mother of James the younger and Joset, and Salome."[8] The public ministry of Jesus lasted approximately thirty months yet Mark doesn't mention Mary of Magdala until the day Jesus died. But Mark tells something of great importance: the women watching used to follow Him and look after Him when He was in Galilee. So, Mary of Magdala had known Jesus since shortly before or after His baptism by John, for Scripture says that Jesus came from Nazareth 'in Galilee' to the Jordan to be baptized. Her call to follow Jesus may have antedated the call of Andrew and Peter (still called Simon). 'Following' in Scripture has the connotation of commitment. When one 'followed' a prophet or spiritual leader, one had accepted, approved of, and believed in the teaching of such leader. So Mary, in addition to providing material aid, had experienced a spiritual conversion and made a decision to follow Jesus.

The Gospel of Matthew, in agreement with Mark, recounts that some women were at Calvary, watching from a distance, the "same women who had followed Jesus from Galilee and looked after Him. Among them were Mary of Magdala, Mary the mother of James and Joseph and the mother of Zebedee's sons."[9]

Luke merely reports that the women who had accompanied Him from Galilee saw all this happen (the crucifixion).[10]

All of the Synoptic Gospels indicate the women watching from a distance. Apparently no male apostles were present. Previously, Peter had denied Him, John had run away, Judas Iscariot had committed suicide. There is no other information concerning the rest of the Twelve.

John describes the scene near the cross: Mary, Jesus' mother, her sister Mary, wife of Clopas, Mary of Magdala, and himself.

All four gospel writers identify Mary of Magdala's presence at the tomb on Easter morning. As with other Scriptural events, there are areas of discrepancy in the Easter story.

Mark describes the scene as very early in the morning with one young man speaking to Mary of Magdala, Mary, mother of James, and Salome, with the message, "Go tell..." Mark's version depicts the women as "frightened out of their wits" who tell no one. However, the next paragraphs of the gospel recount Jesus as reproaching the eleven for they had not believed Mary of Magdala who had gone to them and told them that she had spoken with Jesus. Some scholars believe that these verses (nine through twenty) are not part of the original manuscripts and may have been appended by someone other than Mark.

Matthew explains that before dawn, Mary of Magdala and the other Mary experienced an earthquake enroute to the tomb where one young man says, "Go quickly and tell..." According to Matthew, the women are filled with awe and joy and meet Jesus who personally issues the mission, "Go and tell."

Luke relates that at dawn, Mary of Magdala, Joanna and Mary, James' mother, went to the tomb, saw two men in brilliant raiment who announced, "He is risen."

The Synoptic writers agree upon a very early morning event either just before or during daybreak. They disagree about the number of heralds at the tomb: one vs. two. They disagree upon Joanna vs. Salome as the third woman. They agree about the essence of the message, "He is risen, go tell..."

John's account is longer, more specific. He recounts that while it is still dark, Mary of Magdala came to the tomb and upon finding it empty, ran to tell the others that the Lord had been taken away. Then Mary, Peter and John leave for the tomb. After Peter and John return home, Mary sees two angels in the tomb. Then she encounters Jesus. Initially she fails to recognize Him until He calls her by name. Then she cries out her recognition, "Rabbuni." Jesus tells her, "Go and find the brothers and tell them…" Mary went and told the others.

Despite the discrepancies, Mary of Magdala is cited by all four Gospels as the primary person to whom the news of the Resurrection is given. There has been much discussion among theologians, patristic writers, scholars and historians concerning Mary of Magdala's primacy in the Easter events.

Hippolytus, Bishop of Rome (170-235 A.D.) gave Mary of Magdala the title "Apostola apostolorum" - Apostle to the apostles. This appellation became part of the Byzantine Liturgy.

Cyril, Patriarch of Alexandria (370-444 A.D.) expounded the theory that Christ, by selecting Mary of Magdala to announce His resurrection, had honored all women and had negated the 'sin' of Eve. He taught that Eve, by answering Satan, had ushered sin into creation, and that Mary of Magdala, by greeting Jesus, had ushered redemption into creation. Mary of Magdala had cared for Jesus from Galilee through the years of His ministry. She had not betrayed, denied nor abandoned Him, had watched through His crucifixion, burial, had recognized Him as the risen Christ. How then did this faithful companion become the symbolic epitome of female sinfulness redeemed?

Luke relates the story of a woman "who had a bad name in town."[11] Jesus had been invited to the house of Simon, a Pharisee. An unnamed woman of questionable repute brought an alabaster jar of ointment, wept over Jesus' feet, wiped the tears away with her hair and anointed His feet with ointment, kissing His feet. The Pharisee thought to himself that if Jesus really were a prophet, then He would know what a bad name she had and would not have allowed her to touch Him, because to be touched by an unclean woman would have made Jesus ritually unclean. But Jesus, perceiving the Pharisee's attitude, offered a parable concerning forgiveness of sin. Jesus told Simon the pharisee that because of her contrition, her many sins had been forgiven.

Following this event, in the very next verse, Luke lists the women who traveled with Jesus and provided for Him. Mary of Magdala is, as usual, listed first. The women are described as having been cured of evil spirits and ailments. Mary has had seven demons expelled. Luke continues to tell of Jesus traveling through towns and villages preaching, calming the storm, ousting demons, speaking in parable and performing miracles. It is most unlikely that the unnamed woman, forgiven of many sins, who anointed Jesus, is the same woman who is identified in the very next Scriptural verse, which is however a new chapter, indicating most likely, a different location and a different cast of characters. The public ministry of Jesus lasted approximately thirty months. According to some Biblical scholars, the anointing by the woman with the bad reputation occurred during the tenth month of 28 A.D.[12] more than a year before the passion and death of Jesus.

Israelites celebrated seven Festivals each year.[13] These Festivals were Passover, Pentecost, Tabernacles, Hannakah, Atonement, Trumpets and Purim. Passover was the first seven days of Unleavened Bread, calculated from the full moon of the first month. It would seem from Scripture that Jesus celebrated three Passover Festivals during His public ministry. The first Passover followed John's baptism of Jesus in the Jordan[14] and the wedding celebration at Cana. It was during this Passover that Jesus expelled the merchants from the Temple. The second Passover followed the beheading of John the Baptist, occurring near the time when Jesus pre-figured Eucharist with the miracle of the loaves and fishes. The third Passover is the festival which Jesus celebrated by initiating Eucharist just prior to his crucifixion. It is this Passover which is crucial to the identification of Mary of Magdala.

At least one other anointing of Jesus by a woman occurred during the public ministry. Mark says that two days before Passover the chief priests and scribes were looking for a way to arrest Jesus.[15] Matthew describes a meeting among the chief priests and elders, just two days before Passover. In each case, the Passover mentioned is the one occurring just prior to the death of Jesus. Matthew and Mark place the anointing just two days before Passover in Bethany at the house of Simon, a leper. Neither writer identifies the woman who enters the house, pours very expensive ointment over the head of Jesus. In each case consternation over the cost of the ointment is expressed and Jesus explains that she is anointing Him for His burial. In each story, immediately following the event, Judas Iscariot arranges for his betrayal of Jesus.

As usual, John's story varies in some detail from the others. His event occurs six (rather than two) days before the last Passover of Jesus. It would appear to have happened at the home of Martha and Lazarus of Bethany since Martha is serving dinner. Mary brought in some very costly ointment and anointed the feet (not the head) of Jesus. Again, Judas complains about the waste of money and Jesus tells him that Mary had to keep this scent for His burial. In a previous chapter of his gospel, John had identified this Mary as the sister of Martha and Lazarus, making her Mary of Bethany rather than Mary of Magdala.

So, were there two anointings: the woman with a bad name at the home of Simon the Pharisee, and Mary of Bethany, sister of Martha and Lazarus at her own home? Or were there three anointing: one at Simon the Pharisee's by the woman with a bad name plus one at Simon the leper's house by an unnamed woman and one at Lazarus' house by Mary of Bethany? And where does Mary of Magdala fit in any of these events?

Some early writers believed Mary of Magdala was Luke's sinful woman. Others believed she was Mary of Bethany, sister of Martha and Lazarus. Still others described her as the companion of Jesus, who later preached Jesus risen.

One fact should be self-evident. Other than Mary of Nazareth, mother of Jesus, Mary of Magdala is the only woman listed by name in each of the Synoptic Gospels and also in the Gospel of John. She is not identified as someone's mother, daughter, wife, or widow, as is common in Scripture. She is simply 'of Magdala'. There is nothing in Scripture to identify Mary of Magdala as a prostitute or a 'fallen' woman. If one examines Luke's description of "Mary surnamed Magdalene" from whom seven demons had gone out, one must remember that the expulsion of demons or devils was the idiom used to explain many diseases. Luke, in an earlier chapter,[16] described the expulsion of an 'unclean devil' from a man who was possessed. The people who witnessed the event were astonished by the miracle, but there was no allegation of sin or sexual misbehavior. Jesus expelled many 'devils' throughout His ministry with no hint of sexual or sinful guilt attached to the person cured. So why was Mary of Magdala, from whom seven demons were expelled, depicted as sexually sinful?

The homilies of Gregory the Great (540-604 A.D.) who was Pope (590-604 A.D.) sealed her fate. He identified Mary of Magdala as Luke's sinful woman. He conflated the woman with a bad name with the seven demons expelled from Mary of Magdala. Furthermore, he explained the seven demons as the seven capital sins. So, Mary of Magdala, who had ministered to and faithfully followed Jesus from Galilee to Calvary to Easter to the new Pentecost, became the female embodiment of every vice. The only role left to Mary of Magdala was one of repentance.

Origen (185-254 A.D.) had depicted the sisters of Bethany as models for female spirituality. Martha, busy with many things, became the ideal for women who had chosen an active life. Mary, who had chosen to sit at the feet of Jesus and listen to His teachings, represented the 'better part', the ideal for the contemplative life. Now, this Mary of Bethany was linked with repentant women who anointed Jesus.

But like so many other aspects of the Magisterium, there were dissenting voices. Gregory of Tours (c538-594 A.D.), historian to the Frankish peoples, taught that Mary of Magdala went to Ephesus and spent her life with Mary of Nazareth and John, the beloved disciple. Modestus, Patriarch of Jerusalem (c630 A.D.), claimed that Mary of Magdala was a teacher, a virgin and a martyr.

Devotion to Mary, which began as early as the third century, existed in the Byzantine, Coptic and Syrian churches. She was venerated in Switzerland, Germany, France, Italy and England.

Ironically, by conflating Mary of Magdala with the sinful woman, the feminine Eucharistic symbol of blood and water persists. As a 'sinful' woman, ritually unclean, Mary becomes the 'menstruous woman', the blood. Her tears with which she washed the feet of Jesus, become the water.

As an Apostle, Mary of Magdala was entitled to 'Apostolic Succession.' As the Catechism teaches," Holy Orders is the Sacrament of the apostolic ministry. It is for bishops, as successors of the apostles to so hand on the gift of the Spirit; the apostolic line"[17] Yet Rome still insists that the Lord chose only men to form the 'college of apostles' and that this apostolic succession structures the whole liturgical life of the Church.

It is interesting to note that in the daily Roman Missal, dated February 16, 1937, the Gospel reading for Mary Magdalene's feast on July 22, is that of Luke, chapter seven wherein the woman with a bad name in town anoints Jesus. Following the reforms initiated in Vatican II, the Gospel reading for Mary's Feast is that of John, chapter twenty, the Easter account when Mary receives the mission of the risen Jesus, "Go tell…"

Mary of Magdala, primary among the apostles reminds one of the ancient priest of Genesis, Melchizedek, king of Salem, who was introduced to all through Scripture, had no known father, no known mother, no known ancestry, no apparent beginning or end. He was the first Scriptural person to be called 'priest'.

Mary of Magdala, who was introduced to all through Scripture, had no known father, no known mother, no known ancestry, no apparent beginning or end. She was the first Scriptural person to be called 'apostle' to the Risen Christ.

"You remember that Melchizedek, king of Salem, a priest of God Most High, went to meet Abraham, who was on his way back after defeating the kings."[18]

You remember that Mary of Magdala, follower of Jesus, Son of God Most high, went to meet Christ, who was on His way back after defeating death.

"Woman, why are you weeping?" John 20:13

Paul

Jesus and Saul of Tarsus shared about two decades of time on this earth. Jesus, probably an adolescent when Saul opened his eyes at birth, was born in Bethlehem, a tiny village in the Judean hills south of Jerusalem. Saul was born in Tarsus, a Greek city on the river Cydnus, near the Mediterranean Sea. Previously an important Greek city-state, Tarsus became part of the Roman province of Cilicia. It was a vibrant population center, terminus of major trade routes, with a university that surpassed that of Athens in philosophy and in general education.[1] Saul was Jewish, a descendant of Benjamin, son of Rachel, whose tribe was called by Moses, "Beloved of YHWH". Saul's father was a merchant of Tarsus, weaving cloth and goat hair into tents, carpets, sails and other items common to the time. Saul learned his father's trade and practiced it during his lifetime.

Saul had the unique experience of belonging to three different cultures: Jewish, Roman, Greek. Hebrew was his native tongue but he was fluent in Greek, speaking, reading and writing in that language. Although Saul was Roman citizen, a privilege uncommon among Hebrews, he was Jewish in education, philosophy and lifestyle. As a Jew, Saul was influenced by the theocratic history of Hebrew culture. Jerusalem, which had been the spiritual, political and geographic capital of Judaism for centuries, existed as a population center as early as the fourth millenium B.C. It had been a Canaanite stronghold, conquered by King David. King Solomon built the first Temple there (c970-931 B.C.). Later Jerusalem fell to the Babylonians and the Temple was destroyed. The second Temple was built while Jerusalem was part of a common-wealth under Persian rule (537 B.C.) During the second and first centuries B.C., Jerusalem was the capital of the Maccabees, a Jewish family who wrested Hebrew culture from the Hellenizing and alien influences of Alexander, the Ptolemies and the Seleucids. The Maccabees resanctified the desecrated Temple (165 B.C.). This event is now commemorated by the Jewish Festival of Hannukah. As a Hebrew boy, Saul learned the history of his people: a people chosen by YHWH to follow monotheism and await a Messiah, devoted to preserving their faith, their Covenant, their priesthood, their Temple. They were frequently besieged by alien cultures and spent long periods in captivity or exile. Usually they were distrusted, scorned, victimized and ostracized by their conquerors, including the Romans. Saul, obedient to the Torah, strictly adhered to all Jewish laws concerning prayer, festivals, sacrifice, circumcision, diet, virgins, menstruous women, disease, ritual cleanness versus uncleanness, orphans, commerce and death. During Saul's lifetime there were

Sally Moran

about six thousand Pharisees, Saul's family among them. In addition to the precepts of the Torah, Saul obeyed the many Pharisaical laws preserved through the oral tradition. The Pharisees, theologically orthodox, respected by many of the Jewish community, were strict observers of the Law as well as followers of a substantial body of tradition. The Pharisees were more conservative than the Hasidim. Any contact with a Gentile was absolutely forbidden. Saul distrusted and hated any alien influence which weakened monotheism or his Jewish way of life.

During Saul's lifetime, Jerusalem was occupied by Rome under Tiberius (14-37 A.D.), Caligula (37-41 A.D.), Claudius (41-54 A.D.) and Nero (54-68 A.D.).

Rome, situated on the hills above the Tiber River, safe from the malarial fever which plagued the surrounding lowlands, was the capital of an empire which extended west beyond Spain to the Irish Sea, south to Africa, north to present-day Germany and east to Persia. The wealth of the Empire found its way to Rome. It was a noisy, crowded city, reached by tree-lined roads, filled with sun-drenched temples, patrician tombs, impressive villas, imperial palaces, artisans' shops, hovel-filled slums, and arenas which ran red with the blood of humans and animals.

Fourteen aqueducts carried millions of gallons of pure, fresh water to its inhabitants, daily. It was a metropolis filled with people strictly organized into classes. The patrician aristocracy initially controlled all government. Now, in Saul's time, a senatorial oligarchy still attempted to guide the reins of government, which were manipulated by the commander-in-chief-leader-Emperor Tiberius. The patrician and senatorial classes held enormous wealth and the power which usually accompanies it. Beneath the patrician class were nobles of the second class (equites) who were in military service and whose power rested exclusively upon the amount of money they controlled.

A major part of the population was plebian, the general body of Roman citizens. And of course, there were the large uncounted masses of slaves. There were personal slaves, domestic slaves, theater slaves, prostitutional slaves, agricultural slaves, gladiatorial slaves. The slave had no legal status, being regarded as the property of the owner. Rarely, slaves could obtain their freedom by buying it, through the owner's good will, or as a reward for outstanding service.

Somewhere within this stratified social culture, the Roman female existed. Uncounted in the census (like the slave), generally excluded from inheritance rights, unable to initiate civil proceedings in court, rarely educated, she was married soon after menarche to a man selected by her father. Naturally, such women would hear and embrace the message of freedom, respect and love preached by the followers of Jesus.

Class dissension permeated the culture and exploded into revolts by slaves in 133 B.C., 103 B.C., 73 B.C. These insurrections were consistently squelched through brutal massacres. After the revolution led by the gladiatorial slave, Spartacus, (73 B.C.), six thousand slaves were crucified along the Capua-Rome highway.

Within the civil service of Rome, further classes existed. Quaester (magistrates), praetors (judges), censors supervised public behavior, directed public works, counted citizens, filled vacancies among senators and equites.

Even Roman Law was stratified. 'Legis actis' utilized an ancient script format of charge and refutation. 'Jus civile' concerned itself with Roman inhabitants, while 'jus gentium' dealt with foreigners. 'Jus honarium' was the law which dealt with commerce. It is interesting to note here that Rome's system of laws became the basis for the Canon Law of the Roman Catholic Church.

Saul's father enjoyed the privilege, rare among Hebrews, of full Roman citizenship. And Saul inherited this cherished position. As a Roman citizen, Saul was immune from the extremes of 'justice' legally meted out to foreigners.

But Saul was also Greek. He was born and grew to adulthood in Tarsus, a city which rivalled Athens for Greek culture. Greece, land of gleaming buildings, azure seas, acres of olive trees, god-filled mountains, created a legacy which is still evident two millennia after Saul's lifetime. Archaeology demonstrated that Greece existed since the Neolithic Age, circa 10,000 B.C. By 2,000 B.C. important population centers and culture had developed. By the fifth century B.C. Greece had developed sculpture, architecture, philosophy, drama, poetry, literature, mathematics, medicine and a pantheon of deities. It was in Greece that the concept of democracy was born, although the Greeks, like most other cultures of the time, retained slaves.

Alexander the Great spread the Greek civilization throughout the known Western World, across southern Asia to India. Greek language became an international language, common to most people. But constant internecine warfare among the city-states weakened Greece. In 146 B.C., Rome conquered the Greek city-states, which were allowed to keep their intellectual and artistic pursuits but succumbed to Roman political and economic policies.

Saul, a product of three cultures, demonstrated their influences throughout his life.

As a Pharisee and a Roman, the concept of Law was uppermost in his mind. The Torah and the Law of the Pharisee provided Saul with the stability of YHWH among the proliferations of deities extant. The multiplicity of codes directed every facet of his behavior. Such rules lent order, predictability and rigidity to his days and justified his rejection and persecution of the followers of the Nazarene. Paul said of himself, "as for working for religion, I was a persecutor of the church; as far as the Law can make you perfect, I was faultless."[2] The social structure and the laws of Rome delineated each person's place, rights (or lack thereof), and function. Each person knew his or her role and did not deviate from it without negative consequences. The brutality exercised by the military under the Emperor against any and all malfeasance was counter-point to the Levitical Code which utilized capital punishment against a host of offenses, including the preaching of Jesus as the Messiah.

The depth and breadth of Greek philosophy and literature challenged Saul to reach beyond the narrow confines of the prescribed legitimacy of Judaism and Rome. A more unlikely candidate for Apostleship would be hard to find.

Scripture describes Saul's presence at the execution of Stephen, the first Christian martyr.[3] He 'entirely approved' of the killing, and was instrumental in the bloody persecution which followed.[4] Saul, the Pharisee, furiously angry with the followers of Jesus, had sought written commissions from the High Priest. These commissions authorized Saul to go to synagogues in Damascus to arrest and prosecute any and all Christians. It was enroute to Damascus that Saul experienced a call from Christ.[5] The event changed Saul's life utterly and forever.[6]

For three days after the dazzling heaven-sent light blinded Saul (henceforth Paul), he neither ate nor drank. It was as if he were in some dark tomb. What confusion and guilt he must have experienced while in such darkness. To use Paul's own words, "I am a Jew…taught the exact observance of the Law of our ancestors."[7] He had persecuted the Nazarene and His followers, convinced of the absolute integrity of his ways. Now he knew the Nazarene was everything those mad Christians had claimed Him to be. Afterward, Ananias, a disciple of Jesus, baptized Paul. As sight returned to his eyes, light filled his soul, wiping away all the legal minutiae which had governed his life.

Paul, the converted Jew, preached Jesus, the Son of God.

Paul, the converted Pharisee, evangelized Gentiles, eating, praying, living with them.

Paul, the converted Greek, developed and wrote a body of theology upon which much of Christianity rests.

Paul, the converted Roman citizen, eliminated all class dictinction between people and stressed freedom from law.

Paul released all from physical circumcision, believed by many to be a gender-specific rite. He freed females from ritual uncleanness. Paul told believers that they were 'rid of the Law'. And in order to explain the concept, Paul used a woman as an example.[8] In his letter to the Romans, chapter seven, Paul explained that a woman has legal obligations to her husband while he is alive. If she gives herself to another man, she becomes an adulteress. But, after her husband has died, she can marry again without becoming an adulteress. Paul further explained that Christians, now dead to the Law, can give themselves to a new husband, Christ. This concept became a cornerstone for monasticism.

The earliest Christians, formed into small communities where all assets were owned in common, shared with one another according to need, disregarding any social, economic or hierarchical position. The Jewish Christians met daily in Temple or Synagogue to pray, but met in 'house churches' for the Ritual Meal. Pagan converts also met in the homes of leading Christians for the sharing of the Ritual Meal. They exhibited mutual respect and demonstrated equality in all aspects of daily living. According to Roman Law, such behavior was flagrantly illegal. But Paul taught, "All baptized in Christ, you have all clothed yourself in Christ, and there are no more distinctions between Jew and Greeks, slaves and free, male and female, but all of you are one in Christ Jesus"[9] This message demonstrated how radical Paul had become, not only within his own era, but within himself. Paul, caught up in the Spirit, sensed that everyone, without exception, was loved, forgiven, free, equal before God. Paul repudiated both the Law of Leviticus and the Law of Rome. Looking back across the centuries, Paul's quotation seems to be merely politically correct. But a person hearing it two thousand years ago would have been appalled. It was seditious, dangerous, an infringement of religious and civil law.

Paul was converted to preaching Jesus within a decade following the Christian Pentecost. The memories of Jesus were vividly alive. Christ's life and behavior were present within the experience of His disciples and apostles, both female and male. The women who had followed Jesus from Galilee and had looked after Him were still alive. The many women for whom Jesus had worked marvelous signs were available to recount their experiences. Their gratitude, joy and awe were a constant witness to all. The woman cured of a twelve year bleeding problem, the daughter of Jairus,[10] the now-erect woman whom Jesus had cured on the Sabbath,[11] Peter's mother-in-law,[12] the woman who was no longer a sinner,[13] the widow of Nain,[14] Mary, the mother of Jesus, the Samaritan woman, Mary of Magdala, and the countless unnamed others, were present to the community of faith. The evidence of Jesus' love, respect, empathy, and, His commission to these women, was very obvious. Paul, so close to Jesus in time, could not misconstrue the message of Jesus. And Scriptural evidence indicates that he did not. Many women assisted Paul in the early church. Their roles were varied, not limited by the usual restrictive social and religious customs. Paul speaks of their services in his writings. He mentions females who were deacons, leaders of prayer, teachers, martyrs. He cites females who risked their lives to save him, who served time in prison with him. He names a female apostle.

Paul does not support the concept of a male-only priesthood.

Lydia

Lydia, the first recorded European resident converted to Christianity, was born in Thyatira. Thyatira, located in the northwestern section of present-day Turkey, was conquered by the Hittites in approximately 1800 B.C. and became known as Lydia. Following the fall of the Neo-Hittites, Lydia grew into a small but wealthy empire, and was the cultural and political center of Asia Minor for several centuries. It was a rich land boasting minerals, flax, olive groves, and vineyards which produced a hearty wine. Considered to be rich in gold, Lydia is credited with the first use of gold and silver coins probably in the seventh century B.C. The Persians conquered Lydia in 546 B.C.

Lydia, who carried the name of her birth country, lived in Philippi, an important city of Macedonia, a Roman colony. Philippi was a station on the lucrative caravan routes to Rome in the west or to Byzantium and the Orient in the east. Lydia, a worker in textiles, traded in purple dye. This was one of the more profitable occupations because the wearing or use of purple textiles was restricted to persons of great wealth or to royalty. She conducted her business on the caravan route between Rome and the lands of the east. It is not known whether Lydia was Jewish or pagan, but she is described as a devout woman, who met to pray with the Hebrews every Sabbath. A center for polytheistic cults, there was no synagogue in Philippi, so the Hebrews usually met outside the city walls, near the river, for Sabbath prayers. There, Lydia listened to Paul, and Scripture says, "The Lord opened her heart."[1]

Within some time she and her whole household were baptized. Lydia invited Paul and his companions to stay at her home. Apparently Lydia was an assertive women for Luke (the probable author of Acts) said, "She would take no refusal." It seems that Paul became quite comfortable at Lydia's because after his release from prison, Paul stayed for a while at Lydia's house. There they met with all the Christian community, shared prayers and discussions. Most likely, Lydia's house became an early home church, a place of prayer. As the woman of the house, Lydia would have prepared, blessed and served the Ritual Meal, the Eucharist.

Although Paul usually refused to accept financial support from the Christian communities, Lydia was an exception. She helped to support Paul throughout his ministry.

Damaris

Athens was inhabited as early as the Bronze Age, about the fourth millennium before Christ. In its heyday, it was the cultural and artistic center of the known world. It was also the epitome of intellectual life. Although its strength and glory waned during conflicts with Rome, it still maintained philosophical superiority during defeat.

When Paul was preaching in Athens, he was speaking with well educated philosophers. Many of these people considered Paul's teachings to be outlandish. When Paul spoke of the resurrection of Jesus, some of them burst out laughing. But others became believers. Among the believers was "a woman called Damaris"[1] The fact that Damaris was identified by name indicates that she was notable. Wealthy Greek wives usually lived in seclusion, according to the custom, while poor Greek women were usually ignored. But Damaris was acknowledged. She was singled out as the only female present at the meeting of the Council of Areopagus. Areopagus was the high council of Athens, which regularly convened on the Areopagan Hill. She, and a male, Dionysius, the Areopagite, were the only two persons identified by name among those who became believers. Most likely the woman, Damaris, was a member of the Council of Areopagus. Such membership would explain her presence at the meeting and the use of her name.

It is most interesting to note that Damaris, a woman, and Dionysius, a man, were both identified as converts to Christianity. Such identification demonstrates the absence of gender bias among the followers of Paul and the early Christians.

Priscilla

It is apparent from Scripture that Priscilla was a person of significant value within the early Christian community. Her primacy is evident from the fact that in references to Priscilla and her husband, she is usually listed first. Such practice is most unusual since husbands customarily took precedence over the wives. In Corinth, Priscilla, also called Prisca, and her husband Aquila, worked with Paul.

Corinth, a major port, trading hub and architectural center, was one of the largest, most powerful and wealthiest cities of ancient Greece. Priscilla and Aquila were Jewish Christians who had relocated to Corinth after Emperor Cladius (41-54 A.D.) had expelled all Jewish persons from Roman provinces. They were tent-makers and for a while, Paul lived with them, plied his trade with them, met in their home church for the Ritual Meal and held debates every Sabbath in the synagogue.

Eventually, Priscilla, Aquila and Paul sailed to Ephesus and settled there, where they met Apollos, a Jewish Christian from Alexandria. Located at the northern extremity of the Nile, on the Mediterranean Sea, named for Alexander the Great, Alexandria was a busy, wealthy port, primary center for Jewish and Hellenic cultures. It maintained libraries and a museum whose reputation attracted noted scholars. The school of medicine at Alexandria taught various sciences, including anatomy and mathematics. According to Scripture[1] Apollos was an eloquent man well versed in Scripture, who preached with great spiritual intensity. But, Priscilla gave him further instructions in Christianity. The fact that Priscilla taught Apollos demonstrates her superior position in the Church at Ephesus and accentuates her advanced knowledge of Christianity.

In 1st Corinthians,[2] Paul sends greeting to Priscilla and to the church which meets at her house. As a leader of a 'home church' Priscilla's work would have included preaching, teaching, presiding over the ritual meal, Eucharist, as well as functioning as a mentor and patron for other believers.

In his letter to the Romans,[3] Paul describes Priscilla as 'a fellow worker in Christ Jesus who risked death to save my life...' By calling Priscilla a fellow worker, Paul describes her as a colleague...an Apostle? Paul continues by saying that 'all the churches among the pagans' owe a debt of gratitude to Priscilla. One cannot know what the debt of gratitude entails but the term 'all-the churches among the pagans' certainly indicates some behavior, decision or teaching of significant value.

Scripture assigns various roles to Priscilla: a tentmaker, wife, teacher, Pauline colleague and risk-taker who saved Paul. Most likely, Priscilla was an elder (presbytera), a role which evolved into ordained sacerdotal ministry within the Roman Church.

Some writers allege that Priscilla was the author of the anonymous Letter to the Hebrews.[4]

Phoebe

Cenchraea was a busy port city located on the Saronic Gulf quite near to Corinth. In Cenchraea the Christian community was served by a deacon named Phoebe. According to Paul, she looked after a great many people, a large congregation, which included both females and males. In older Scriptural translations, Phoebe is described as having 'assisted many.' The Scriptural language demonstrates that Phoebe's ministry was not gender limited. Although some scholars maintain that female deacons, called deaconesses, ministered only to females, such was not the case with Phoebe. Paul calls Phoebe a deaconess of the Church, his sister, one who has looked after many, himself included. Paul further discussed Phoebe in his letter to the Romans, which was written about 57 A.D. It is accepted by scholars that Phoebe was the deliverer of this letter. Being the bearer of an epistle from Paul was a great honor and a significant responsibility. Although it is difficult for the twenty-first-century-cyber-literate person to visualize, personal delivery of written correspondence was the only means of long-distance communication in the years immediately following the Resurrection of Jesus. Correspondence from Paul, who was revered as the evangelist of the Gentiles, the one who challenged Peter face-to-face, was of prime importance. And Paul entrusted delivery of this letter to Phoebe. No doubt Phoebe also had additional responsibilities on that particular trip to Rome, because Paul directs the Roman Church community to give her a warm welcome and 'help her with anything she needs.'

Phoebe was most probably a wealthy widow. Such social status would have enabled her to work and travel as she did, since the trip from Cenchraea to Rome was long and costly whether one took the sea route or traveled overland. Furthermore, Phoebe was most likely a patron of the community as well as a deacon.

In early Christianity, three degrees of sacerdotal service developed: the episcopate, presbyterate and the diaconate. The episcopate evolved into the position of bishop, the presbyterate into the priesthood and the diaconate into the deacon. By the second century all three levels of hierarchy were in general use. Within the first several centuries of the Church's history, the three ministries were not gender limited, as evidenced by Scripture. Paul identifies women who were co-workers, apostles, deacons.

In the first epistle to Timothy, not necessarily written by Paul,[1] qualities for both female and male deacons are listed. They were expected to be conscientious believers, respectable, sober, quite reliable. In the third century, Origen, leader of the catechetical school at Alexandria, identified Phoebe as the basis for apostolic authority for female deacons as an ordained female ministry within the Church. Some scholars believe that Phoebe became the initiator for a 'regular order' of female deacons.[2] Lator, John Chrysostom (347-407A.D.), Patriarch of Constantinople, who was no great advocate for women, interpreted Paul's letter to the Romans as validation for ordained female deacons. His opinion was offered in the latter part of the fourth century So, conservatively speaking, for at least four hundred years, it is an historical fact that women, such as Phoebe and others, functioned as deacons, an ordained office of Holy Orders, within the Roman Catholic Church.

During the Middle Ages the ordained priesthood was divided into Minor Orders and Major Orders. From the late Middle Ages the Minor Orders and Major Orders were considered to be incremental steps to the priesthood. The orders in ascending fashion, were: doorkeeper(portress or porter), lector, exorcist, acolyte, sub deacon, deacon, priest.[3]

Following the reforms of Vatican II, Pope Paul VI (1963-1978) restored the office of deacon to a permanent, independent order with its own ministry: preaching, baptizing, and distribution of Holy Eucharist. The restored diaconate is limited to males, negating Scriptural and Traditional and Magisterial precedents for a dual gendered diaconate.

Chloe

Corinth, the wealthy, beautiful, pagan city in which Paul, Priscilla and Aquila worked before moving to Ephesus, was the area where Chloe, whom Paul mentioned in his letter to the Corinthians, labored for the Lord. In addition to the usual exports of olives, grapes, wine, and the common imports of spices, dyes, silks, the people of Corinth imported fantastic philosophies and sought novel experiences. The sophisticated Corinthians posed a serious intellectual challenge to the message of the Cross. Paul had enjoyed only minimal success among the Jewish Corinthians and moderate success among the Corinthian Gentiles. The fledgling Christian community there encountered many problems in leaving pagan customs to follow the Nazerene. Within a short time they broke into rival factions. Chloe's people described to Paul the serious differences among them.[1] Some supported Paul, some Cephas, some Apollos. Was this Apollos the eloquent preacher taught by Priscilla? Were the dissensions along theological lines? Philosophy was of significant prestige in Corinth and it may have contributed to the lack of cohesiveness among the Christians there.

But there were further serious problems among Chloe's people. Some relapsed into idolatry, eating food in pagan temples, practicing prostitution while others lived in incest and some committed fornication and pederasty. Liturgical disputes among the Christian Corinthians had disrupted their Ritual Meals and in their hostility to one another, they had resorted to litigation in pagan courts.

Apparently the situation among the Christian community in Corinth was out of control. "Chloe's people" brought all of this information to Paul. It is evident that Paul, in his letter to the Corinthians, expected the Christians there to know who Chloe and her people were.

Who was Chloe? What was her role? Was Chloe an elder, a preacher, a prophet? Or was she one of the leaders like Paul, Cephas, Apollos? Who were Chloe's people? Were they her deacons? Were they her congregation? While none of this is known, we do know that Paul, in his letter to the Corinthians, indicates her importance. In reiterating and expounding on the theology of the Eucharist, on spiritual gifts and virtues, as well as on the problems identified by Chloe, Paul supported Chloe and validated her concerns for the Christians in Corinth.

Junia, Apostle

In 57 A.D. or 58 A.D., Paul wrote his letter to the Romans, the letter which Phoebe, the deacon of Cenchraea, probably delivered. When Paul wrote this letter, the Christian community in Rome was mostly Gentile with a Jewish minority. In chapter sixteen, Paul introduced Phoebe; sent greetings to Priscilla, his colleague who had worked with him in Corinth and Ephesus, and to Mary, a hard worker. He saluted the mother of Rufus who had been like a mother to him, and Julia. He mentioned many persons in this letter, both female and male.

And Paul also greeted those "outstanding apostles, Andronicus (male) and Junia (female).[1] Paul did not use the word 'apostle' freely. He limited the term to those who had been with Jesus and borne witness to the resurrection. In order to explain his own mission, he had referred to himself as an 'apostle appointed by God.'[2] It is, therefore, notable that he called Junia not only 'apostle', but an 'outstanding apostle'. Paul noted that Junia had received the Holy Spirit before he had. One wonders was she with Jesus from the time when John was baptizing and was Junia present in the upper room at

Pentecost?[3] If not, then Paul had found other reasons for calling her apostle. Evidently she preached Jesus and witnessed to the Resurrection, sufficiently active and notable to merit imprisonment, for Paul called her a 'fellow prisoner.' He also called her 'compatriot', a term which would indicate that she was Jewish. Was she of his own tribe, of Benjamin? Or perhaps she originated from his birthplace, Tarsus? Junia was a common female name in that area at that time. For more than ten centuries there was no doubt concerning the female gender of this apostle, Junia. Origen (c185-254 A.D.) of Alexandria was the most outstanding Christian theologian of his era. An Egyptian Christian, he had studied under Clement of Alexandria and was the chief apologist of the catechetical school of Alexandria. He authored hundreds of treatises, exegeses and letters in theology, philosophy and Scripture. His writings are still utilized as references in the new catechism. Origen accepted the female gender of the apostle Junia.

Jerome (c340-420 A.D.), a Father and a Doctor of the Church was a renowned Christian scholar. He translated much of the Bible into the Latin vernacular as well as some of the works of Origen. Jerome composed commentaries on the Epistles of Paul, and he also accepted the feminine gender of Julia. John Chrysostom (344-407 A.D.), another Doctor of the Church, one of the great Greek Fathers of the Church, was a Patriarch of Constantinople. His writings include homilies and treatises on Biblical interpretations and the priesthood. His oratory was such that he was called 'Chrysostom', which means golden mouth in Greek. And this Doctor, Father, Patriarch, orator, accepted the female gender of Junia.[4]

Centuries later, Hatto (924-992 A.D.), Bishop of Vercelli, wrote the Capitulare, a noteworthy dissertation containing instruction for the clergy. Hatto was an advocate for general education who loathed superstition. Among his many literary compositions was a commentary on the Pauline Epistles. He too accepted the female gender of Junia.

Theophylactus (1050-1105 A.D.), Archbishop of Ochryda, was a Byzantine prelate, scholar and exegete. He authored commentaries on the Synoptic Gospels, the Gospel of John, the Acts of the Apostles, the Minor Prophets and the Pauline Epistles. He, like others, accepted the female gender of Junia.[5]

As an apostle, Junia, like Mary of Magdala, should have been included in Rome's 'apostolic succession' which, according to the catechism "structures the whole liturgical life of the Church".[6] However, Aegidius of Rome (1245-1315 A.D.) changed the name of Junia to Junias. He thus changed the gender of an apostle from female to male, a concept also popularized by Martin Luther. By this arbitrary and misleading change, Rome destroyed a vital link in the Scriptural foundations for female ordination. In so doing, Rome perverted Scripture and betrayed more than twelve hundred years of Tradition.

Paul, so often maligned as misogynist, demonstrated throughout his lifetime that females were worthy of, and expected to serve in, all levels of ministry. Paul made "every effort to preserve the unity which has the Spirit as its origin and peace as its binding force."[7]

There is not even any hint of gender bias in that statement.

What Is an Apostle? What Is a Priest?
Can Women Fulfill the Role?

The word 'apostle' comes from the Latin word 'apostolus' and the Greek word 'apostulos' meaning 'to send' An apostle is a delegate, an ambassador, the one who is sent. In the Scriptural New Testament sense as defined by Peter[1] an apostle is one "who has been with us the whole time...from the time when John was baptizing until the Ascension and who can act as witness to the Resurrection." In the strictest sense, only one person meets these criteria. Mary of Magdala was with Jesus from Galilee (when John was baptizing), she witnessed to the Resurrection and was present until, and after, the Ascension.

The Church defines an apostle as one who was called by Jesus; taught and presided over the community; spoke in the name of Jesus; performed signs and wonders in His name.[2]

75

Sally Moran

According to Jesus, criteria for apostleship are commission, service, poverty and love.[3]

All three definitions agree on a call, a commission. Throughout the ages, persons of both genders have heard that call. And they have responded: fearfully, bravely, eagerly, reluctantly. They were/are prophets, clergy, royalty, peasants, warriors, healers, persons from every walk of life, women and men.

Although Scripture sometimes uses the term 'disciple' and 'apostle' interchangeably, it has been generally accepted that Jesus called twelve male apostles. Of that twelve, Judas betrayed Jesus, Peter denied Him, and John ran away during crisis. In chapter ten, Luke recounted how Jesus appointed seventy-two other followers and sent them ahead of Him in pairs (wives and husbands?) to "all the towns and places he himself was to visit." The seventy-two came back rejoicing because of their success. The use of the term 'others' rather than men, brethren or apostles, is most interesting. More than likely, this group included the women who had been with Him since the beginning. But when the Church speaks of Apostolic Commission / Succession, this incident is conspicuously absent. Usually, Apostolic Commission refers to the pre-Ascension scene related by Mark (16:14-20) and Matthew (28:16-20). Yet, when Jesus gave this 'Apostolic Commission' there were only eleven men present and, at that time, Jesus reproached the apostles for their obstinacy, the rufusal to believe Mary of Magdala's message.[4] Then Jesus said, "All authority in heaven and on earth has been given to me. Go, therefore, make disciples of all nations."[5] Since only eleven men were present for the momentous event, it is quite reasonable to believe that the other, the twelfth, place, vacated by Judas, was/is open for other apostles whom Jesus called: Mary of Magdala (female), Paul, Tabitha (female), Barnabus, Andronicus, Junia (female), Patrick, Bridget, Xavier, Cyril, Methodius, Jeanne d'Arc, as well as Matthias, who was chosen by the casting of lots.[6] This commission of the eleven is indicative of Jesus' intention to include Jew, Gentile, female, male, free person or slave in the Apostleship of the kingdom of God.

In Luke (8:1-3), in addition to the Twelve, certain women accompanied Jesus, making their way through towns and villages. They met Peter's definition of having been with Jesus the whole time.

76

Unlike many women in Scripture, some of these women are identified: Mary of Magdala, Joanna, Susannah. Scripture does not recount how they were called but the fact that they were traveling with Jesus and the Twelve indicates some interaction between them and Jesus, some invitation and acceptance. These women, called by Jesus, were present with Him throughout His ministry[7], His crucifixion,[8] and His burial.[9] They fulfill Peter's next criterion: witness to the resurrection. According to Scripture, there were no witnesses to the resurrection, except perhaps for the Roman soldiers assigned to guard the tomb. But, the women were at the tomb very early on Easter morning. "And they remembered His words"[10] - that He would rise again. Matthew identifies these women as "the same women who had followed Jesus from Galilee."[11] Mark also relates the story of the women who had followed and looked after Him since Galilee.[12] He agrees that they were present at His death, burial and on Easter morning. John mentions only Mary of Magdata in his resurrection account. On Easter morning, Jesus came to meet the women, greeted them and said, "Do not be afraid..."[13] This constitutes commission. The very first persons commissioned by the risen Jesus were also the first to witness to the resurrection, all of them female. These women thus fulfill all of Peter's Apostleship criteria: "with us the whole time" and "witness to the resurrection."

Women also fulfill the following Church criteria: called by Jesus; taught and presided over community; spoke in the name of Jesus. The women who were at the tomb on Easter morning told of the resurrection to the eleven males and to all of the others, female and male, who were convened in the upper room. These women were thus teaching and speaking in the name of Jesus as would the women who participated in evangelization with Paul and others following him. According to Scripture (Acts of the Apostles and Paul), women presided over communities, fulfilling another Church criterion for apostleship. However, we have no Scriptural record of signs and wonders performed by females, as is the case for most of the eleven male apostles.

How do the Church's criteria for apostleship differ from those of Jesus? Jesus' criteria are fewer but far more profound. Jesus' criteria: commission, service, poverty, love. Mark, Matthew[14] and Luke[15] describe Jesus' sending the Twelve: do not go to the pagans or Samaritans; proclaim the kingdom of heaven; cure the sick; raise the dead; cleanse lepers; cast out devils; take no gold, silver, copper; bring no luggage, clothing nor shoes; be cunning as serpents, harmless as doves. You have received as gift; give as a gift. This original commission was limited to the Israelites, but in sending His disciples to the sick, leprous, ritually unclean, Christ shattered ancient but persistent concepts and broke with tradition. Furthermore, Jesus called the commission 'gift'. "You have received without charge, give without charge." Other translations of this passage say, "The gift you have received, give as a gift."[16] The message of Jesus is clear: do not limit the gift by any bonds, gender or otherwise. It was not Jesus' plan to restrict salvation solely to the Israelites for He told the eleven apostles to preach to all nations. Neither was it Jesus' plan to restrict sacerdotal ministry to Israelite males. As shown earlier, Jesus called and sent (commissioned) women as well as men.[17]

The next apostolic criterion set by Jesus is service. John tells of the theme of service in his account of the Last Supper.[18] The women who traveled with Jesus were service oriented. Matthew, Mark and Luke all describe these women as having "looked after Him." Even at His death, they were faithful to service, arriving near daybreak to anoint His body. John[19] reiterates the importance of service when he quotes Jesus, "No servant is greater than his master, no messenger is greater than the one who sent him." Matthew[20] also gives the same message of service: "A disciple is not above the teacher nor a servant above the master." Jesus ministered to all whom He met. He taught, fed the hungry, forgave penitents, cured physical, spiritual and psychological ills. He never sought wealth, power or honor. He said, "The Son of Man has nowhere to rest his head." That message is evidently lost among the silk, gold, wealth and power flagrantly manifest among the male hierarchy throughout history.

Matthew, Mark and Luke describe the scene where the male apostles are aguing among themselves about who is the greater[21]. In each telling the message of Jesus is clear: service - the least is the greatest.

Another Jesus-element of apostleship is poverty. What of the women who traveled with Jesus? Did they practice poverty?

Matthew[22] tells of the "same women who had followed Jesus from Galilee and looked after Him." Mark[23] says, "There were many other women there who had come up to Jerusalem with Him. Luke describes the women as traveling with Jesus and the twelve and providing for them out of their resources, spending their own funds to provide for Jesus and the apostles.[24] Most likely, these women initiated the practice among Christians that is described in Acts:[25] holding everything in common. John[26] says that Judas Iscariot was in 'charge of the common fund'. These women held nothing back for themselves, leaving all to follow Jesus. They most certainly fulfilled Jesus' standard for poverty.

The last and most profound apostolic attribute mandated by Jesus is love:

> "Go and be reconciled."[27]
> "If someone…would have your tunic, give your cloak as well[28]
> "Love your enemies, pray for those who persecute you[29]
> "You must love your neighbor as yourself."[30]
> "This is my commandment: love one another as I have loved you."[31]

Jesus used very strong language concerning love. His love was emphatically gender-free. Thus, in excluding persons of female gender from full participation in the ordained ministry, the Vatican continues its prejudicial posture, in direct contradiction of Jesus' message of love.

The women of Scripture fulfilled Jesus' mandate. The women of Scripture met all of Jesus' criteria for apostleship: commission, service, poverty and love.

Most importantly, there is nothing in the criteria for apostleship - not in Peter's, not in the Church's, not in Jesus' -which indicates gender specificity. So too, with priesthood.

In early history, the office of priest or shaman was attained via one of several methods. In some cultures the role was inherited. The king, chief or tribal leader transmitted the office to the candidate. In other cultures, where the tribal leader and the shaman was one office, priesthood was achieved through whatever means conveyed power. In still other situations, an aspirant for the office of priesthood experienced a spiritual cognition or calling, and after successfully enduring a time of trial, the candidate achieved the state of priesthood.

In many cultures, tribes were led spiritually by female shamans.

In the Old Testament, particularly following the Exodus, the priests were of the tribe of Aaron, who was a Levite[32] and all were male. Such gender limitation was most likely a reaction against the pagan bias in favor of priestesses. In early Judaism there were three priestly functions: service of the Oracle (interpretation of prophecy and tradition), service of the Law (Torah), and offerer of Sacrifice. In the New Testament, the term 'priest' was rarely used except in relation to ritual cleanliness,[33] or to illustrate that the letter of the Law is subject to human need, because the Son of God is master of the Sabbath.[34]

Jesus did not use the term 'priest' for Himself nor for any of His followers, perhaps because in Jesus all three elements of the Old Israelite priesthood merge. Christians believe that Jesus is the fulfillment of prophecy; Jesus is the fulfillment of the Law (all authority is given to Him); Jesus is the perfect and everlasting sacrifice.

The term 'priest' to identify the celebrant of the Lord's supper was not in use until the latter part of the second century following the death of Christ.

In early Christianity, the Ritual Meal, Eucharist, was held in home churches of women who prepared and served the meal. Most likely these women were the first persons to be called deacon. The definition of 'deacon', which came from the Greek: diakonos -to serve, also included ministry to others, and eventually, was used to denote traveling missionaries. Paul used the term to describe himself, as well as Phoebe of Cenchraea,[35] and there is ample evidence that females and males held the title and fulfilled the role of deacon.[36]

Within the early church of Christianity, the term 'presbyter' eventually evolved into the title 'priest'. The term 'presbytera' indicated a female and the term 'presbyteros' indicated a male. A rather wide body of evidence demonstrates that women in early

Christianity held the title 'presbytera' and that they performed all priestly functions They baptized, preached, blessed the bread of Eucharist.[37]

The Preface for the Chrism Mass[38] celebrated during Holy Week, gives the Christian definition of priest: the priest is called by Christ to share in His sacred ministry, to renew the sacrifice of redemption in Jesus' name by setting out the Paschal Meal; to lead His people in love; to nourish them by His word; and to strengthen them through the sacrament.

All of the qualifications listed in the Chrism Mass are met by the women of the New Testament. As deacons of the emerging Church, they set out the Paschal Meal and they certainly led in love as attested by Paul, the Synoptic Gospels and the Gospel of John. They were the very first persons to announce the Risen Lord and they strengthened His people through the sacraments.

Furthermore, the women of today, active in the many ministries of the Church also fulfill all the duties of the priest enunciated during the Chrism Mass.

Scripture certainly supports women as apostles and as priests.

Sally Moran

PART II

TRADITION

Sally Moran

INTRODUCTION

Jesus said, "How ingeniously you get around the commandment of God in order to preserve your own Tradition." Mark 7:9-10

Tradition is the link connecting the present with both the past and the future. It contains lore concerning religious, social and cultural development. Originally passed orally from each generation to its successor, Tradition includes creation and god-myths, heroic legends, delineation of roles and standards for conduct for daily life. Because it comes from the past, Tradition cannot be changed, but the recording of Traditional behavior can be altered or suppressed.

Paramount within religious tradition are symbols and rituals involved with sacrifice, and the many types of behavior associated with spiritual beliefs. Within the Jewish Tradition it is believed that God gave the Israelites two forms of teaching: oral and written. Written Jewish Tradition is chiefly contained in the Torah, which includes the Hebrew Scripture. The records of oral teaching as it was transmitted and debated by Jewish scholars from ancient times to the Middle Ages is called the Talmud. The Talmud represents a sacred deposit of more than two thousand years of Jewish reflection, law, legend and philosophy.[1]

Within the Roman Catholic Church, Tradition includes the teachings of the Apostles and the early so-called Fathers of the Church, originally transmitted orally, but eventually written. Other contributions to Catholic Tradition include, "liturgical books, ancient titles, sarcophagi, frescoes, etc. the most imposing collection of which is to be found in the catacombs."[2] The pronouncement of Church Councils and the writings of theologians and Doctors of the Church, which are considered to be Magisterium, are also part of Tradition, as are rites, rituals and symbolic representations.[3]

John Paul II claims that his position against female ordination, "has been preserved by the constant and universal Tradition of the Church." But, Church Tradition has been neither constant nor universal. It has evolved. As Vatican II teaches, Tradition makes progress within the Church. Therefore, evolution, growth and maturation are implied. Scripture, Tradition and Magisterium are interrelated and interdependent. They are also parallel in time, each reaching back into antiquity, influencing the present and projecting forward into the future. Unfortunately, Tradition within the Church, initially freed from Patriarchy by Jesus and Paul, soon fell under the negative influences of Greco-Roman misogyny. Once again, women were perceived to be inferior beings, naturally and morally subjective to men, a source of sin. Ensuing centuries witnessed the gradual intensification of patriarchal repression of females within the Church. Instead of a collegial relationship, teaching and baptizing all nations, women were systematically and incrementally excluded from any position other than servitude and child-bearing. Traditional behavior, culture and expectations became defined by restrictive customs.

In the infant Christian Church, Peter, without the intervention of Paul, would have clung to an ancient and exclusionary Tradition. Peter would have limited the Gospel to the people of Israel and perhaps most of the world might never have heard the message of Jesus. Now, the Vatican, like Peter, clings to an interpretation of Tradition which is invalid. But, unlike Peter, the Vatican will not listen to any other approach. Jesus, the centrality of Christianity, never ordained anyone, but He did commission females as well as males. Jesus said, "Mary has chosen the better part and it shall not be taken from her."[4]

Sadly, for all females, it has been taken away.

RELIGIOUS SYMBOLS

Creator and creation myths are the building blocks of every culture. They have endowed both female and male genders with divinity. Although varying somewhat from one geographical area to another, nothing better demonstrates humanity's unity than the consistencies which appear throughout mythology. So too with the symbols and rituals related to humanity's interaction with its Creator-Sustainer.

For eons humanity stumbled around seeking the Creator-Sustainer. Some primitive peoples conceptualized God as an Omnipresence to be feared and placated. Ancient pagans, through their spells, incantations, potions, amulets, runes, divination, sought to magically manipulate the Divine since much of their relationship with their gods was fear-filled. Other tribes sought knowledge of and unity with the Divine.

Religious symbols cross geographic, ethnic and cultural divisions. According to Webster, a symbol is "a concrete representation of moral or intellectual quality. From the Greeks, a token."[1] Religious tokens (tree, fire, stone, animals, circle, grain, water and blood) are distilled from the archaic remnants of humanity's common memories. Long before oral tradition was reduced to writing, people saw in these symbols aspects of the Divine.

The symbols discussed here are limited to those still utilized in the Roman Catholic Eucharistic Liturgy. It is interesting to note that none of these symbols is considered to be exclusively masculine. Yet, Rome continues to exclude females from presiding at Eucharist, maintaining, erroneously, that Christ selected only males to be Apostles.

Tree

From the current Great Britain across Europe into Asia, and throughout Africa and the Americas, the tree is a major religious symbol. For the Polynesians, the tree stood at the gates of the land of those who seem to be dead but are living and those who seem alive but are dead.[2] It carries green living branches on one side, but dead, sere branches on the other.

An Icelandic Edda describes a tree, "The Eddic World Ash" named YGGDRASIL, upon which the great Norse god, Odin, hung for nine days, suffering from a spear-inflicted wound.

In Siberia, shamans believe that the tree, "TUURU", is the site wherein the shaman's soul is reared. The shamans believe that God created two trees, a female, the fir, and a male, the larch.[3] For the Celtic and Teutonic tribes of northern Europe, followers of Druidism, the Sacred Grove of Oak Trees was the seat of the divine. African tribes have God's Tree, Buddhists their Tree of Enlightenment, Sumerians their Tree of Truth, the Mayans their Tree of the World. For the monotheistic faiths, there is Eden's Tree of Life. The tree, a living entity, having roots within the earth, limbs stretching heavenward, harboring animals, reptiles, insects and birds, is a microcosm of creation.

The tree is a dual-gender symbol.

* * *

Fire

Fire is a symbol used throughout history, on every continent. Around 7,500BC, a fire-myth from the land now called New Guinea, told of a boy emerging from the body of a serpent bearing a fire-brand with which he started a fire and cooked a meal for himself and his sister. Eastern fire-myths describe fire as a gift (in some cases, the body) of a goddess. The hearth goddess, Fugi, is included in the name of Japan's volcano, Fujiyama. In Hawaii, Pele is the fire goddess of the volcano. In ancient times, especially in Europe, fire was believed to protect our ancestors from evil spirits or demons. In Ireland, during the winter solstice, fires were lit on every hill and kept burning until dawn in order to dispel the darkness and induce the return of the sun. During the early Middle Ages, sacred fires were maintained in monasteries, faithfully tended by nuns. The Roman Catholic Church still blesses the 'new fire' from which the paschal Candle is ignited during the Solemn Easter Liturgy. Fire, source of heat and light, is symbolic of faith, love, enlightenment, purification.

Fire is a dual gender symbol,.

* * *

Rock

Natural rock or stone formations have long symbolized the presence of deities. Earliest idols were carved rock figures. The totems of the native Americans and the Australian Aborigenes are not unlike the standing stones of Europe, Africa and Asia. The Apa Tani tribe of Eastern Asia adored natural rock formations as the seats of spirits,[4] while tribes in the Americas, Africa, Asia and Europe built sacrificial sites composed of rock or stone. These ancient sites frequently became the foundations of later ziggurats, pyramids, temples, mosques, cathedrals. Rock is symbolic of strength, constancy, power.

The earliest rock icons were exclusively female. Later, the standing stones were considered to be phallic symbols, producing dual gender symbolism.

* * *

Animals

Animals have long been major symbols in all areas of the world. The Israelites sacrificed both female and male animals in purification rituals. The Evangelists of the New Testament are symbolized as an eagle, calf, lion and man. One century after the death of Christ, the fish became a symbol of Christians. In Medieval art Jesus was portrayed as a stag.[5] When not worshipped as actual deities, animals symbolized various virtues such as wisdom, strength, speed, fertility, peace.

89

Animal symbolism is dual gender.

* * *

Circle

The circle is an image which like the Creator-Sustainer, is without apparent beginning or end. Its shape represented the moon goddess/god and the sun god/goddess. From circa 3,200 B.C. the circle represented the heavenly orbs: Mercury, Venus, Mars, Jupiter and Saturn. Due to such symbolism, temples, ziggurats and cities were planned in circular patterns.

Among some American native tribes the circle symbolized the ever watchful eye of God. Calendars were devised in a circular shape representing the circle of the horizon and the dome of the world. The circle is still found in the prayer wheels of Asia, and in Eastern art it is reflected in the golden haloes found in icons. In current Christian practice, the circle is apparent in the Advent Wreath and the Communion wafer. The circle represents eternity, fullness of being, completion. The circle is a dual gender symbol.

* * *

Grain

Grain reached enormous stature in religious significance. The lowly grain - corn, oat, rye, barley, wheat, rice - is ubiquitous in symbolism. An element so vital as seed mandated a deity of enormous power. The earliest deities were powerful females, goddesses of religions based upon fertility. There were grain priestesses in Africa and the Americas and corn maidens throughout Europe.

Nearly every bread is made from flour obtained by grinding grain, and throughout history, in most cultures, the original planters and grinders of grain were female. Both European and Asian cultures assigned feminine symbolism to grain, as was done with most seed bearing plants.

Grain is the elemental ingredient of bread, the staff of life, with its own significance in every culture. There are ceremonial breads for most social events, such as wedding cakes, birthday cakes, funerary breads. Bread represents food, security, hospitality, health.

Bread is considered to be feminine.

* * *

Water

Water is an ubiquitous symbol throughout history. From the devastating flood waters of the Deluge to the 'holy' water hawked at religious shrines, water has been an emblem crossing geographic and ethnic boundaries. "Water is the vehicle of the power of the goddess."[6] It is considered by many to be the source of life. Genesis states that even before there was light, there was "wind sweeping over the waters."[7]

In Great Britain, Ireland, Europe holy wells, sacred pools and springs are still venerated. In Africa and Asia millions ritually bathe in the holy waters of sacred rivers. In Judaism, a convert must be immersed in a ritual bath, and Christians need baptism to become initiated into the congregation. According to evolutionary theory, life began in primordial sludge originating in the sea.

Water, representing life, fertility, cleansing, birth, is considered to be a feminine symbol.

* * *

Blood

Blood, integral to the maintenance of life, can be the agent of disease and death. One of the most pervasive of religious symbols, it is an essential element of ritual in Africa, the Americas, Australia and Europe. Across many centuries, on every continent, countless animals, women, men, children and infants have been deliberately slaughtered in order to spill their blood before a host of deities.

Throughout history, blood has been feared by tribal men of all continents, particularly the blood of childbirth and menstruation. Elaborate rituals and rules for purification from female blood were formulated thousand of ages ago in Africa, Asia, the Americas and Europe. Such behavior most likely contributed to the harsh patriarchal traditions of history.

The very word "blood" signifies many concepts: bad blood (emnity), blue blood (aristocracy), blood bath (carnage), bloodshed (murder), blood curdling (fear-filled). Blood, the coin of contrition, atonement, redemption, consists of approximately three-quarters water.

Although blood flows through the circulatory systems of both females and males, like water, symbolically, it is essentially feminine.

In many rituals, wine represents blood. Roman Catholics profess that, within Eucharist, wine becomes the blood of Christ.

EUCHARIST

The tradition of offering sacrifice is part of humanity's history on every continent, in most cultures, through all ages. People indulged in sacrifice to avert disaster, appease the gods, save the community. Sacrifice was also offered to promote healing,[1] to give praise and to cleanse or sanctify. It was an act of love or hope. Sacrifice as atonement sought to recreate equilibrium between the Creator-Sustainer and humankind. Through sacrifice, humans attempted to commune with the Divine, become united within the Cosmos. Left to their own devices, humans indulged in excessive, orgiastic, sometimes brutal sacrifice. For example, Scripture says that Solomon sacrificed twenty-two thousand oxen and one hundred twenty thousand sheep as a peace offering in just one ritual.[2]

Sacrificial offerings included fruits, vegetables, grains, animals, beverages, jewels and humans. Human sacrifice may have evolved from economic values since in many cultures a slave, criminal or a captive was worth less monetarily than an animal. In several cultures, criminals were routinely sacrificed because state and religion were one. Human sacrifice included slaves, felons, prisoners of war, infants, first-born sons, virgins, and, rarely, a king. Australian Aborigines sacrificed their first-born sons in order to ensure additional sons. The Mohicas of Peru sacrificed healthy youths, collected their blood into sacred cups and offered the libation to their goddess. The Pawnees sacrificed a virgin to the Morning Star and the Mayans offered products of the harvest plus jewels and animals. In extreme need, such as drought, human sacrifice was practiced. The Aztecs waged war in order to provide sufficient humans for sacrifice. The handsomest and the bravest prisoner of war was selected, dressed lavishly, treated royally for a year, then led to the sacrificial site where he was beheaded. His heart was cut out and eaten by the shamans while the rest of his body was consumed by other members of the ceremony. By treating one of the victims like a king, the shamans hoped to elevate the value, hence the power, of the sacrifice. Aztecs killed hundreds of persons at each ceremony.

The ApiTanis of Asia sacrificed a chicken, dog and a pig which were consumed during the ritual meal. In Africa, sacrifice included animals, beer, hens, brandy, and in rare instances, the African Anlo tribe sacrificed a virgin. Through consumption of the offering, participants believed that they became united, if only for an instant, with their god.

The sacred meal involved the sharing of an offering between the Divine and human. In most cultures, the offering (whether vegetable, animal or human) was treated with respect prior to sacrifice. In some cultures, the victim was sedated with fermented grain or herbs, to reduce possible fear or anxiety. In other tribes, a ceremonial ritual permission was obtained. Among the ancient Greeks, the sacrificial animal was greeted, stunned and then killed. It was cut into portions, wrapped in fat and barley, and placed in the fire. Wine was served. The meat represented nomads, the grain, farmers. After some wine had been sprinkled on the ground for the gods, the participants drank wine themselves and consumed the meat and grain. Although the sacred meal sought to link the profane world with the realm of the Divine, remnants of the sacred meal have remained in the profane. Nearly all cultures celebrate various social events around a meal or a banquet. In sports, victory celebrations involve champagne and a meal. In social and business interactions, people meet for lunch or dinner. In Western culture, holidays are celebrated with lavish meals. In monotheistic lore the first sacrifice is recorded in Genesis[3] with no indication of the ritual or the site. Genesis says that Cain offered produce from his land and Abel offered first-born animals from his flocks. In religious practice, the sacred meal as sacrifice still persists. Among the Jewish people, annually at Passover, the Seder Meal is consumed to commemorate the liberation of the Israelites from Egypt. For this rite lambs were sacrificed until the Temple was destroyed.[4] The lamb recalled the nomads, the unleavened bread, the agrarians. Other symbols recalled the haste with which the Hebrews were forced to flee Egypt, remembrance of the Covenant, and unity among believers.

The Christian Eucharist Liturgy evolved from the Passover Meal. Jesus, at His Passover Meal, initiated the Eucharistic Meal. Christians believe that Jesus is the sacrifice, the celebrant, the God. Jesus, believed by Christians to be the Word of God made human, was sacrificed. Atonement, the need for equilibrium between the Divinity and humanity, was completed, once for all, for Jesus accomplished what countless shamans and priests had striven for from the dawn of history. And this was-is-accomplished within the ultimate sacrifice of the Christians, the sacrament of the Eucharist.

For believers, a sacrament is a sign, one that points backward through our history and our memory. It also points forward through faith and hope to the ultimate union with love and joy in God. But a sacrament is more than a sign, for within sacrament an action takes place within the human spirit-soul which enhances the YHWH/Word/Spirit presence within the human soul.

Baptism utilizes the ancient universal symbol of water, which represents life, birth, cleansing. Reaching backward, baptism reminds one of Noah, of the water poured from the rock for the Israelites in the desert, of Jesus immersing Himself in the Jordan. In baptism, the spirit-soul of a person is cleansed and grafted onto the vine which is Christ.[5] In baptism, one becomes part of a chosen race, a royal priesthood, a consecrated nation, a people set apart.[6] Jesus, speaking with the eleven apostles, said, "Baptize in the name of the Father, Son and Holy Spirit."[7] Baptism confers new life in Jesus. There is no gender limitation here. The sacrament of baptism has been conferred on females and males since the time of the apostles and the sacrament of baptism may be bestowed by persons of either gender.

Confirmation too reaches far into the past. In ancient traditions, oil was burned in lamps as a source of light. Oil, used cosmetically to enhance beauty and medically to ease pain, was poured upon the heads of queens and kings to seal their royalty. Oil is symbolic of health, joy, cleansing. In Confirmation, the candidate is anointed with blessed perfumed oil, called chrism. The candidate for Confirmation frequently selects an additional name to demonstrate an enhanced identity, an enhanced sense of mission. Sarah's name was changed by YHWH to demonstrate her new identity, her commission, her holy order to participate in the Covenant. Confirmation reaches back to the Christian Pentecost when the Holy Spirit-Breath of God vivified both females and males in the Upper Room. Confirmation is everyone's Pentecost, wherein one participates ever more deeply in the

Priesthood of Christ. Once confirmed, one has been anointed, has had a 'laying-on' of hands, is compelled to speak out and share one's faith with others since one is filled with the Holy Spirit.[8] Like the Samaritan Woman, who, once she realized that Jesus was the Messiah, hurried back to the village and shared her 'good news' with everyone, all are ordained to spread the 'good news' - the Gospel. Confirmation is bestowed upon females and males. The Holy Spirit knows no gender restrictions.

Eucharist, too, looks back into history, recalling the long persistent struggle of humanity to be united with its Creator. Eucharist, believed by Christians to be the perfect sacrifice, is the nourishment of one's spirit throughout life. Through Eucharist, Christians are united with God and with one another. Both genders are permitted to participate in Eucharist. However, Rome still restricts consecration of Water, Wine(blood) and Bread at Eucharist to males.

Eucharist is the culmination of humanity's struggle, aching, and yearning for perfect sacrifice, and Eucharist utilizes humanity's ancient symbols:

> The dual gender tree is represented in the wood of the cross
> The dual gender flames of the candles recall the fires of Moriah, Sinai and Carmel where YHWH called Israelites from idolatry
> The fixed altar is constructed from natural stone and recalls the dual gender rocks of antiquity
> The many animals sacrificed throughout the ages are recalled when Christians refer to the Lord as 'Lamb of God'
> The dual gender circle and the female gender grain are present in the Communion wafer
> The female gender water is used for ritual ablutions and is mixed with wine in the chalice
> Blood is present in the consecrated wine
> Together, water and wine recall Jesus' gender specific (female) symbol: Water and Blood

Once again, God stoops to humanity's symbols to present the ineffable sacrifice, the Word of God, as mere bread and wine, mixed with water. Bread is not exciting. It is staple, boring, commonplace. But the act of bread-making is almost mystical. Combine flour, water, yeast, knead and give the dough time to rise. Soon the dough expands, alive, aromatic. It expresses the essence of food, the staff of life. Homemade bread is thick, crusty, chewy, wholesome. Store-bought bread, mass-produced, plastic-wrapped, thin-sliced, loses its sense of bread. So too, the communion wafer. It too is mass-produced, stiff, low-taste, low bread-sense, low mystic sense, "Truly, God is hidden with you."[9] But like bread-making, faith, hope, love (the Holy Spirit breathing within) act like leaven to expand and enliven the congregation.

Wine, unlike bread, is not staple, not boring. In some cultures it may be commonplace, while in others it is rare. But, like the grain which becomes bread, wine is the result of planting, growing, harvesting, grinding, mixing and maturation. Then wine too becomes vibrant, aromatic. Wine in the Eucharist is like the kiss of God on one's lips.

Eucharist is accepted by believers as covenantal sacrifice in which the agent, offering and the god are one. The priest represents Christ. The bread and wine (mixed with water) become Christ. Christ is One with the Father and the Holy Spirit. Eucharist crosses ethnic, geographic, temporal and gender barriers. In Eucharist, all (priest, offering, congregation) become One. One becomes all. Eucharist encounters YHWH, the unnamable One. YHWH made a Covenant with humankind, summoned Sarah, Hagar, Rebekah, Leah, Rachel, Miriam, Zipporah, Rahab, Ruth, Huldah, Elizabeth, Mary, Hannah, Anna, Susanna, Naomi, Mary of Magdala, Martha, Esther, Junia, Phoebe, Chloe, Lydia, and countless other women. YHWH promised, "I will be your God and you shall be my people." Eucharist is the fulfillment of the Old Testament prophecy, "That brings peace, and through his wounds we are healed."[10]

Yet the Vatican, in apparent contempt for Jesus' mandate, bars access to ordained Eucharistic ministry (Holy Orders) to females. Holy Orders is the only Roman Catholic Sacrament limited to males.

Sally Moran

WOMAN IN CHURCH TRADITION

The status of woman has risen and fallen throughout history. Before approximately 2,300 B.C., in Egypt, Sumer, Minos and in some of the lands north of the Mediterranean Sea, women enjoyed inheritance rights, education, social and political powers. Many women were leaders in their political and religious institutions. Eventually their position declined in North Africa and in the Mid-East, most likely due to Babylonian and Assyrian influence. By 1,700 B.C., under the Code of Hammurabi, the situation worsened.

The Hebrew culture reflected the international social decline. Hebrew women lost inheritance rights and were considered to be the property of men. Women were stoned or burned for adultery, while guilt was rarely ascribed to the male. Polyandry was explicitly forbidden in Hebrew Law, but polygyny was not. The male was permitted to own many female slaves, keep concubines, marry many wives. He could divorce the female but the reverse was forbidden. Around 650 B.C., after centuries of failure to eradicate pagan goddess cults from the Israelite culture, Jewish male prophets sought to discredit goddesses by using the female as the symbolic epitome of evil. Around 612 B.C., the prophet, Nahum, decried "that wonderful beauty, that cunning witch who enslaved tribes by her spells.[1]

In other cultures, the status of women continued to decay. From the Indus Valley through Egypt to the Mediterranean lands, women's social position reached an extremely unfavorable level following the conquests by Alexander the Great, pupil of Aristotle (384-322 B.C.). No doubt Aristotle's theory that women were naturally passive, hence naturally subordinate, influenced Alexander who was largely responsible for the spread of Hellenic culture throughout the Near East and part of Asia. Females, given in marriage shortly after menarche to men chosen by their fathers, were expected to provide children for their tribe or the empire. There were few other options.

Alexander's influence reached into the already restrictive Hebrew culture. By the time Jesus lived, Jewish men were instructed not to speak much with women, not even their wives.[2] This attitude was in accordance with the Roman culture, expressed by Pliny the Elder (c

23-79 A.D.) when he said that the work of female physicians was purposely hidden because, "Women should be quiet and inconspicuous as possible so that after death no one would know that they had lived."[3]

Although most Roman, Greek and Hebrew females during the century surrounding the birth of Christ were still forced to marry in their teens, there were other females who agitated for an improvement in female status. Some women had actually succeeded in obtaining liberalization of laws under Augustus (63 B.C.-14 A.D.). Under such laws wealthy widows, freed-women, female artisans were able to avoid marriage and to control their own finances. Such women, relatively independent of male control, functioned within the culture as persons of business, or patrons of those in need of support such as artists or itinerant preachers. The women who followed Jesus, and Paul's convert, Lydia, are examples.

In less than fifty years following the death of Jesus, Christian communities had developed in Jerusalem, Greece, Egypt, Syria and the lands now known as Italy and Turkey. Most of the evangelization of these areas was provided by preachers, traveling on foot, spreading the Good News, praying, prophesying, healing, baptizing, performing exorcism. The original evangelists included the apostles and disciples of Jesus. It is most likely that the women who had followed Jesus from Galilee to Pentecost were among those first preachers.

Dependent upon the charity of those to whom they ministered, the evangelists found respite in private homes which provided hospitality, places for liturgical services, evangelical interaction. Such centers of faith became known as house (or home) churches. An example of the importance of such places is the Roman Church, "Titulus Prisca", built in the fourth century, which occupies the site of the original home of Prisca (Priscilla), Paul's co-worker and colleague.[4] The liturgy practiced in such home churches no doubt varied slightly from culture to culture. But some re-telling of the scenes from the life of Jesus, shared prayer, and a re-enactment of the Last Meal (Eucharist) formed the heart of the service. When a visiting preacher of some renown was present, such person would have been expected to speak to the assembly. But the preparation and distribution of the Ritual Meal remained the duty of the owners of such home churches: Chloe,

Lydia, Nympha, Priscilla, and many other females never identified. These home-churches, centers of worship and liturgy, became the nuclei of the Christian communities and survived as such for two centuries.

As years passed, the apostles, disciples and other contemporaries of Christ aged and died or were martyred, and the burgeoning Christian church began to revert to patriarchal ways. Clement I (88-97 A.D.), fourth bishop of Rome, decided that only a bishop or 'trustworthy' priest could celebrate Eucharist. Later this opinion was echoed by Ignatius (d 107 A.D.), bishop of Antioch.[5] Why 'trustworthy' celebrants? According to some scholars, prophets were the preferred celebrants by many of the communities[6] and most prophets of the early Church were women. The four daughters of Philip, the Evangelist, were prophets.[7] Cyprian of Carthage described a female prophet in Cappadocia who celebrated Eucharist.[8] In Lyons, the prophet, Marcus, concelebrated Eucharist with a woman. Was Clement attempting to undermine the sacerdotal power of the female in the early Church? If so, why?

By the middle of the second century after Christ, hierarchical levels were developing within the Church. Structurally, this hierarchy was quite similar to the Roman Army.[9] The servers (diakonos: both female and male) were the deacons. From the earliest days, the deacon was recognized as an ordained ecclesiastic office shared by females and males. In addition to serving at Eucharist, deacons distributed alms, taught, preached, baptized, carried Eucharist to the sick. Prayers and rubrics for ordination of both genders span the years until the sixth century in both the Eastern and Western Tradition.

Elders evolved into priest. The female elder was called presbytera, the male, presbytero. Ross Kraemer reports that a diverse body of evidence[10] shows that women held the title presbytera and that they performed all priestly duties: teaching, baptizing, consecrating Eucharist. There is a fresco in the Catacomb of Priscilla in the Via Saleris Nova, Rome, which depicts a group of women celebrating a Eucharistic Liturgy. The name of the fresco is "Fractio Panis", Latin for Breaking of the Bread.[11]

The role of overseer evolved into bishop. The female was called episcopa, the male, episcopus. There are mosaics and stone inscriptions in Saint Praxedia in Rome which contain the word, "episcopa", female bishop. These mosaics have existed since the second century after Christ.[12]

The hierarchical structure may have evolved in opposition to the Gnostics, a growing sect which differed substantially from the Bishop of Rome. Among the Gnostics, ranks of persons were not allowed. All practiced equality, especially at Eucharist. The Gnostics cast lots at each meeting to determine roles at Eucharist. A person might act as elder (priest) today or as an overseer (bishop) tomorrow. By casting lots, they eliminated favoritism and power. They believed the lots expressed the choice of God.[13] Although the practice was decried by Irenaeus (125-202 A.D.), Tertullian (160-230 A.D.) and others, there were precedents, especially by Peter, who cast lots to select Judas' successor among the male apostles. But Tertullian may have identified the real problem among the practices of the Gnostics when he protested the participation of "those women among the heretics. They teach, they engage in discussions; they exorcise; they cure."[14] In short, they functioned as bishop. Yet in Tertullian's African Church, the revelations of a female prophet regularly followed the Sunday Liturgy.[15] Tertullian, considered a 'Father' of Latin Theology, who called females "the devil's gateway", eventually severed from Rome, becoming a heretic himself. He became a Montanist, a sect which repudiated a return to grace after contrition for sin. Ironically, the Montanists were led by two female prophets who maintained that the gift of prophecy was given equally to females and males by the Holy Spirit. Surprisingly enough, this 'heretic' is still cited in the New Catechism on issues as divergent as the resurrection of the body, the sacrament of Penance, the Lord's Prayer, abortion, martyrdom, moral law and faith.

In addition to functioning in ordained ministry, females within the early Christian church formed into groups of widows and virgins. They ministered to the sick, lived and prayed in community.[16] These women were attacked from all sides. Roman Law still maintained that women must marry and provide children for the empire. Any who refused were condemned to rape and prostitution. Tertullian suspected that virgins, having eschewed family life, would assume sacerdotal roles. Iraneous, Bishop of Lyons (125-202 A.D.), complained that women were abandoning their homes and parents to follow a life-style that was at odds with a family-centered social structure, a sentiment which is still echoed in Rome twenty centuries later. Yet, among the early Christians, many of whom expected the imminent return of Christ, marriage and procreation seemed superfluous. The desire to leave all earthly pleasures in pursuit of sanctity fostered the growth of the orders of widows, virgins, and the monastic movement.

In the second and third centuries as the structure and power of the hierarchy grew, so did repressive tactics against charismatic, prophetic expressions of faith. Concomitant with the rise of the hierarchy was its thrust toward unification and control of the many congregations. Celebration of Eucharist was moved from the home churches to centralized sites for worship utilizing only male celebrants. Bishops became presiding pastors of major congregations, usually in urban population centers. By the fourth century, within some areas, Ecclesiastic Law ruled that only a bishop could preach. A priest was allowed to preach only with a special dispensation. Obviously, such practice limited the ministerial roles of females within the Church. Furthermore, the bishops developed the concept of 'apostolic succession' which alleged that the original twelve male apostles were the original bishops, hence they (the current bishops) were providing to their congregations the teachings of the Apostles.[17] And included in this teaching was the ability to identify dissenters as heretics.

Additionally, entrance into the Order of Widows became restricted to elderly women, effectively limiting growth of the Order by denying access to younger women. While ecclesiastical assault on female ministry within the church grew unabated, the monastic movement established itself as a viable Christian life-style. Monasticism, an ascetic search for spiritual fulfillment, usually practiced in the desert, was of two major styles: eremitic and cenobitic. The eremitic style involved solitary living, a hermit. The cenobitic life-style consisted of communal living with others of similar spiritual philosophy. Whether eremitic or cenobitic, monastics practiced an ascetic life utilizing prayer, fasting, self-mortification, vigil-keeping, chanting, contemplation and physical labor. By the fourth century, ascetics flourished in Egypt, Syria, Gaul and Palestine.

Interesting to note, female monastics outnumbered males by about two to one.[18]

Cenobitic monasticism initiated the development of abbeys. Originally nothing more than a cluster of huts, the abbeys became centers of prayer and work where women and men led separate but parallel lives, usually under the spiritual leadership of an abbess. The members of the community usually met only for meals which were taken in silence. Both in Eastern and Western Christianity, women who functioned as abbesses were spiritual overseers. And as overseers, they were ordained 'episcopae', female bishops.[19] The rite for ordination of abbesses is still retrievable from several sources.[20] The directions for ordination included prayer, garbing with sacerdotal vestments, presentation of ecclesiastical insignia and prostration before the altar. The sacerdotal (priestly) garb included the alb (an ankle length white cotton or linen dress signifying purity); the stole (a long silken band worn around the back of the neck, crossed over the chest, symbolic of the yoke of Christ).[21] The insignia presented were the crozier (a hooked staff, symbolic of the shepherd's staff); the pectoral cross (worn on the chest, symbolic of ecclesiastic office); the ring, gloves and the mitre (ceremonial headdress similar to that once worn by the Jewish high priest). The crozier, pectoral cross, ring, gloves and mitre were worn only by bishops or higher members of the hierarchy, a custom still in practice today. Like the male bishops, abbesses were expected to exercise spiritual as well as temporal jurisdiction over the persons in their care.[22] Their duties included accepting tithes from the local churches, assigning vicars (priests) to parishes and paying their stipends. The abbesses enjoyed the privileges accorded to the landlords over the temporal estates involved in their abbeys. As landlords, abbesses were allowed to present candidates for ecclesiastical positions thereby influencing parish formation.[23]

Physically, abbeys grew into complete, independent communities consisting of a chapel (eventually a church), a bell-tower, living quarters (individual cells), cloister, choir, refectory, infirmary, dispensary, scriptorium, and work rooms for sewing, weaving, candle-making, leatherwork, cooking. In addition, there were the usual outbuildings involved with farming and animal husbandry.

Monasticism attracted persons from all walks of life. For women, monasticism provided an escape from familial patriarchal control with its mandate for marriage and procreation, and allowed females identities equal to males. Wealthy women gave their fortunes to the service of the church through monasticism, while slaves and freed-persons were allowed to seek sanctity living as equals with persons from families with high social standing. Abbess Macrina, sister of Basil the Great and Gregory of Nyssa, (both Bishops, Fathers and Doctors of the Church) lived in community with her former (freed) slaves and acted as spiritual leader for Basil for over four years while he resided in her abbey.[24] Basil, credited with writing the Basilian Rule for monasteries, no doubt utilized concepts he learned while living under the rule of the house of Macrina. Her biographer brother, Gregory, credited Macrina with providing the model for other monastic communities.[25]

Jerome, Father, Doctor of the Church, translator of the Bible, papal secretary to Pope Damasus, spent the last twenty years of his life living in the monastery of the Abbess Paula at Bethlehem.

Despite the popularity of monasticism, bishops' concerns about powerful females living in communities with males strengthened misogynistic tendencies and confirmed a near-pathological hatred of women. The hierarchy endeavored to compel all male monastics (monks) to accept ordination, further reducing the status of female monastics. Additionally, the Council of Orange, held in 441 A.D., convened by the Emperor Theodosius, which had banned further ordination of deaconesses, was followed by the Council of Chalcedon (451 A.D.) which forbade the erection of any new monasteries without the consent of the local bishop. This action limited any new settlement wherein women and men lived under a common superior, usually an abbess. Although Emperor Justinian effectively suppressed such abbeys in the Eastern Church, the practice continued in the British Isles, France, Spain, and even in Italy.

Patrick (c385-461 A.D.) brought monastic Christianity to Ireland. Bridget (c450-520 A.D., spelled variously as Brigid, Brigit or Brighid), converted by Patrick, became his successor and was renowned for her missionary zeal. She built a monastery at Kildare which was preeminent among Irish monasteries. Cogitosus, a monk of

Kildare Abbey, wrote in his eighth century biography of Bridget, that uncountable numbers of people thronged to her: the sick for healing, the wealthy bearing gifts, the sinner seeking spiritual reconciliation. He also said that Bridget received the pallium (bishop's mantle). Other hagiographers relate that she was ordained.[26] as a bishop. Subsequent to Bridget, the abbesses of Kildare were considered to be peers of the Primate of Armagh (a male archbishop).

Ita, a sixth century abbess of County Limerick, Ireland, who founded Killeedy Abbey, was known as a prophet and a confessor.

Samthann, abbess of Clonbroney, Ireland, was an eighth century leader also well renowned as a confessor. She was known to possess a crozier, a symbol of episcopacy.[27]

Irish monastics are credited with preserving much of European culture during the Dark Ages, (c450-750 A.D.).

In Saxon England, where abbeys flourished, many were heavily endowed by kings and lords. British abbeys covered hundreds of acres of land containing several villages, parishes and the population living therein. The power, wealth and influence of the abbess was on a par with kings, lords and bishops. Present at all major religious and national solemnities, abbesses, like the queen, participated in national assemblies and signed charters, With bishops and civil rulers, they took part in councils and synods. In 694 A.D., at the Council of Becanfield, five abbesses signed the decrees. Hilda, Abbess of Heruten and Whitby, who had founded numerous abbeys, presided at the Synod of Whitby (664 A.D.) which addressed the oft-repeated controversy concerning the proper date for the celebration of Easter.[28] Abbess Hilda was well renowned for the regular discipline of her houses, so much so, that five men of her monastery became bishops.[29] It was known that kings and princes went to her for guidance.

Other famous abbeys existed in the British Isles, all under the jurisdiction of abbesses, ie, Codingham, Barking, Bercingame, Wilton, Nunaminster, Shaftesbury. The Abbess Etheldreda was listed as the Bishop of the Cathedral at Ely.[30]

In Germany, abbesses were considered to be the peers of the princes, and as such, sat and voted in the Diet as members of the "Rhenish bench of Bishops."[31] The abbesses of larger abbeys, such as Quedlinburg, Gandersheim, Lindau, Buchaw, Obermunster, held their own courts, and like most other abbeys, were exempt from all ecclesiastical rule except for that of the Bishop of Rome, the Pope.

French abbeys included Sainte-Croix, Montmartre, Chelles, Laporte. The abbess of Conversano, Italy, appointed her own Vicar-general and authorized priestly functions in churches under her jurisdiction. She regularly received the homage of her clergy. Each member of the clergy approached her, made obeisance and kissed her ring, while she sat enthroned beneath a canopy, wearing her mitre, ring and holding her crozier.[32]

During the Middle Ages (c499-1499 A.D.), some abbesses baptized, heard confessions, preached, read and taught Scriptures, blessed their congregations, consecrated Eucharist. In 1040 A.D., the Abbess of Uberwasser, Germany, was named Archdeacon and Episcopal Vicar for the diocese.[33]

The abbesses of Spain appear to have had the most significant powers. It is interesting to note that the ecclesiastical See of Spain is reputed to be of Apostolic origin, perhaps explaining why the abbesses of this See were the most powerful. The abbess of the Cistercian Monastery of Santa Maria le Real delas Huelgas, Burgos, was officially a 'noble lady' ie the superior prelate and lawful administrator with complete jurisdiction in spiritual and in temporal matters of the abbey, convents, churches, hermitages and villages within the area belonging to the monastery. Like the bishops, she held her own courts, granted letters for ordination, issued licenses to priests to hear confessions and to preach. She was able to confirm abbesses (a rite which was usually reserved to bishops), to impose censures on priests suspected of heresy, and to convene synods. The Abbess of las Huelgas retained these rights until their abrogation at the Council of Trent in 1545 A.D., sixteen centuries after Christ!

In addition to centers of monasticism, the abbeys became sites of vast wealth, with extensive jurisdiction, and the power to confer enviable patronage. Many abbesses were the sisters or daughters of kings, princes or other nobility. Unfortunately, many young women were placed in an abbey by their parents. They had no desire to follow an ascetic life-style. They dressed stylishly, entertained lavishly, hosted guests, hired servants. Some of them traveled away from the abbeys on lengthy visits to families or to friends. Others eloped, still others were charged with pregnancy. Their behavior seriously damaged the reputation of the monasteries. As a result, the female monastics who still practiced the virtues of hospitality, charity, prayer, tending the sick and the aged were also deemed to be corrupt. Such abuses were heralded by the male members of the hierarchy as reason for 'reform'. All too frequently such reform resulted in the abrogation of the rights and responsibilities of the abbess. Gradually the abbess was prevented from administering the land, receiving tithes, managing the clergy and other temporal and spiritual matters. Reform frequently did nothing more than turn the abbey (with its wealth and power) over to male rule. It seemed to many that the day of the rule of the abbess was finally coming to an end.

The bishops, throughout the centuries, had tried many times to subvert the authority and wealth of the abbesses. And the abbesses, many of whom maintained exempt abbeys, appealed to Rome to protect their rights and authority from ecclesiastical incursion. Abbess Oda obtained protection from Pope Leo IX in 1049 A.D. In 1076 A.D., Abbess Gisla of Chamoussey obtained assistance from Pope Gregory VII against the Bishop of Toul.[34] However, the Church of Rome, a powerful civil as well as spiritual institution since the era of Charlemagne (742-814 A.D.), was embroiled in political intrigues for supremacy over imperial monarchs. Members on both sides of the controversy used it as reason for taking the lands and wealth of the abbeys. The Spanish Lord of Bergueda turned 'corrupt' females out of the Abbey of Sant Joan de les Abadesses in 1099 A.D [35] and Philip I sought to give Mar Moutiers 'to the monks' claiming that it had become a brothel.[36] The famous ancient English Abbeys, Ely and Whitby, were turned over to monks. Furthermore, the papacy refused protection to abbeys which were politically supportive of its enemies. For example, in 1119 A.D., Calixtus II excommunicated Abbess Agnes of Quedlinburg and Gandersheim for her loyalty to her king. Abbesses, with their abbeys, dependencies and populations, were enmeshed in the political, theological and social upheavals of the eleventh and twelfth centuries.

In 1074 A.D., Gregory VII excommunicated all married clergy. The independent, permanent diaconate, now exclusively male, was abolished as such and became a stage in preparation for a male-only celibate priesthood. And in 1210 A.D., Innocent III (Pope 1198-1216 A.D.), formally withdrew from abbesses the right to hear confessions or to preach.[37] This transfer of confession from the Abbess to a male confessor weakened the compassionate, intimate, spiritual relationships within the abbey and also deprived women of the spiritual leadership of their own gender. Furthermore, the bishops unsuccessfully sought to prevent nuns from chanting the Divine Office, a spiritual exercise performed by females and males from the third century.

During the thirteenth century, misogynism still prevailed as expressed by Vincent de Beavais, encyclopedist. He explained a woman as "the confusion of man, an insatiable beast, a continuous anxiety, an incessant warfare, a hindrance to devotion."[38] It was during this era that the female gender of the Apostle Junia was changed by Aegidius of Rome (1245-1316 A.D.) to male.[39] This was done despite the fact that Church Fathers, Church Doctors, and Church Teachers Origen, Jerome, John Chrysostom, Hatto of Virceli, Theophylact and Peter Abelard all had accepted the gender of Junia to be female.[40] But this was another segment of the episcopal drive to render females impotent. The medieval males could not accept the concept of a woman as an 'outstanding Apostle'[41] an opinion which still prevails today in some areas of the Roman Church.

In the fourteenth century, many females were persecuted as witches. The charges of witchcraft held peculiar parallels to liturgical practices within the church. A coven of witches was thirteen - the number of the original male apostles plus one, or the usual number of persons chanting the Divine Office plus one. The so-called witches were accused of participation in a black mass - a diabolical Eucharist, supposedly containing bizarre and depraved perversions of the true Eucharistic Liturgy. They were accused of consorting with the devil, infant cannibalism, demonology and a host of other offenses. Of course, since most 'witches' were extensively tortured, they confessed to all sorts of hideous behavior. They were fined, expelled from their homes and villages, tortured or burned alive. The youngest female burned alive for witchcraft was Catherine Naquille, eleven years old.[42] In 1390 A.D., the Inquisition declared witchcraft a heresy after the Council of Chartres (1366 A.D.) declared all sorcerers to be anathema. The "Malleus Maleficarum" (translated as 'Hammer Against Witches) states that all witchcraft comes from carnal lust, which is, in women, insatiable. In 1431 A.D., Jeanne d'Arc was burned at the stake for witchcraft and heresy. Heresy claims a long history in Christianity. From the second century, certain Christians decided that they were orthodox possessors of the truth. They called all dissenters 'heretic' and heresy became an especially common justification for capital punishment.

The fifteenth and sixteenth centuries were times of great turbulence in Europe and in the Church. The Church suffered from a loss of mission. The hierarchy, now entirely male, was corrupt from the Papal Chair down to the village clerics. Religious practices, polluted with superstition, were merchandised like property. The wealthy could buy the Eucharistic Liturgy (the Mass), indulgences, remission of punishment for sins, even Heaven. Cardinal Cajetan, General of the Dominicans, Papal Legate to Germany, commented.

"We, who should have been the salt of the earth have decayed until we are nothing beyond outward ceremonials."[43]

Martin Luther (1483-1546 A.D.), an Augustinian priest-theologian, who was appalled by the spiritual bankruptcy of Rome and the widespread selling of indulgences, spearheaded the massive break with Rome: the Protestant Reformation. In an effort to regroup and to establish dogmatic definitions, the Council of Trent was convened. It was planned so that clarification of issues and correction of abuses could be simultaneously accomplished. It was held during the reigns of three popes. In 1545-1547, Paul III presided. In 1551-1552, Julius III presided, and finally, in 1562-1563, Pius IV presided. The Council of Trent seriously undermined any remaining authority of the abbesses. As a result of this Council, even previously exempt abbeys were placed under the authority of the local bishop. Now, the local bishop was to be seen 'as a delegate of the Holy See'. For many centuries the abbesses (the episcopae) had been the ecclesiastical peers of the bishops. They had received obedience from all persons under their care; had exercised spiritual and temporal authority for all within the abbey's boundaries; had read the Gospel to all; had preached; had heard confession; had been ordained. On the Feast of Christmas 1563, the Council of Trent additionally weakened women by reducing the power of the abbess even further. Under that 'reform', nuns were cloistered and were not permitted to leave the convent without permission of the local bishop. Abbesses were denied the duties and powers which they had held for fourteen hundred years. The Tradition which had existed since apostolic times was destroyed, since the very first group of women who had lived in community had done so while Peter was still alive.[44]

Abbeys, as such, were disbanded. Convents were placed under the Rule of Benedict and all feminine autonomy was lost. Woman's role in the Church became peripheral. Christ's legacy of freedom, dignity and equality for women, which had gradually declined since post-apostolic times, was destroyed. In its place stood the ancient pre-Christian posture: weakness, subservience, uncleanness and shame.

As the Protestant Reformation spread, any Roman Catholic Christian women who still remained within the convents functioned in the only roles left to them: teaching poor women, nursing and serving the marginalized members of society. The role of the woman in Roman Catholic Christianity continued to remain severely limited for centuries. At the cusp of the eighteenth century, females heard sermons which taught: "A good wife is like a mirror…which has no image of its own."[45]

The nineteenth century witnessed the end of all abbesses' rights to any episcopal jurisdiction over the women in religious orders, promulgated by Pius IX (Pope 1846-1878 A.D.).

Women, who had been represented in each level of the original three tiered hierarchy (diakonos, presbytera, episcopa) from the earliest days of Christianity, were aggressively, cruelly and incrementally excluded from any sacerdotal function. The frequently cited "unbroken Tradition" is at best a myth, at worst, an intentional misrepresentation of the truth.

Within the world of religion, exclusive of the Church of Rome, some women advanced. 1853 witnessed the first ordained woman minister in the United States, A.B. Blackwell. In the secular world, females began to break down male-erected barriers. They entered universities, made significant contributions to the arts and sciences.

The twentieth century saw women in many countries organizing and demonstrating for women's rights, especially the right to vote.

But progress for women within the Roman Catholic Church remained paralyzed. In 1929, the Lateran Treaty, signed by Cardinal Gasparin for Pius XI and by Mussolini for Victor Emmanuel III, identified the Vatican as an independent state located within the City of Rome with the Pope as absolute ruler. So, the Holy Roman Empire, which once had ruled from the Mediterranean and Adriatic Seas to the northern coasts of Europe, from Gaul to Byzantine, was reduced to 108.7 acres. The close political ties between Emperors, Kings and the Pope were severed.

In 1930 the Canon Law of Rome still prevented any sister (a woman consecrated to serve the Lord, a nun) from becoming a mid wife,[46] despite the fact that sisters worked in hospitals and also in rural mission areas not served by any physician. At that time, missionary sisters outnumbered missionary priests and brothers combined by a 2:1 ratio.[47] This is the same ratio which existed within monasticism sixteen centuries previously.

In 1955 the Presbyterian Church resolved: "There is no theological ground for denying ordination to women, simply because they are women. In 1958 the Swedish Lutheran Church admitted females to pastoral office.

And in 1962, John XXIII convened the Second Vatican Council. The goal of the Council was intended by John XXIII to open the windows and let fresh air breathe through the Roman Church. It's impact was significant. The renewal of religious life and the reform of the Liturgy brought joy, freedom, sorrow and consternation to the women of the Church. Sweeping changes in the lifestyle of many congregations of consecrated women led to spiritual rejuvenation for some and disillusionment for others. In 1968, the number of female religious in the United States was 176,000. In 1992, the number was 99,000. However, the role of consecrated women in the Church changed significantly. Although many still functioned in the traditional fields of teaching and nursing, others became parish administrators, coordinators of religious education within a parish. Some became physicians, university deans, administrative aides, retreat directors, spiritual directors. Many no longer live in community within a convent. They live independently, work in

111

pastoral care, community outreach, crisis intervention. Some are associated with a parish, others with a diocese.

The role of the Roman Catholic laywoman changed also. Within the Liturgy, some function as cantors, lectors, extraordinary ministers of Eucharist. Others function as directors of liturgical music, as liturgists or as directors of religious education.

1970 was an interesting year. After the passage of almost two thousand years, the Vatican conferred the title "Doctor of the Church" on two women: Catherine of Siena (1347-1380 A.D.) and Teresa of Avila (1515-1582A.D.) Among the multitudes of females who had followed Junia, Phoebe, Tabitha, Priscilla, Mary of Magdala, and others too numerous to name, only two received the title which had been conferred on thirty-two males. Also, in 1970, a Pontifical Biblical Commission study, completed for Paul VI, found no Scriptural basis for exclusion of females from ordination.[48] Although the Vatican never published it, the study had significant influence upon the Church of England's decision to ordain females.

In 1976, the Episcopal Church ordained the first female priest and in 1989 ordained the first female bishop.

In 1994, the Church of England (Anglican Communion) ordained females. But, in that same year, John Paul II issued a letter "Sacerdotalis Ordinatio" which claimed inability to ordain women because of Scriptural reasons, the constant practice (read Tradition) and the living teaching authority of the Church (read Magisterium). That year also saw the Presbyterian Church in the United States (2.8 million believers) elect the first female to its highest Office.

In November 1995, in a statement approved by Pope John Paul II, the Vatican announced that Roman Catholics must consider the ban on ordination of females to be 'infallibly taught'. Rather than put an end to the question, this action has created a "great problem for a lot of individual consciences."[49]

In 1998, the Vatican announced that belief in the ordination of women is an example of a punishable error. Already several women have been denied participation in Eucharist by their local bishops and hundreds have been excommunicated in the United States for daring to dissent. Books advocating ordination of females have been removed from circulation by order of the Vatican.

Traditionally the status of women in the. Roman Catholic Christian Church has incrementally declined since post-apostolic times. The traditional roles assigned to them by Christ and Paul, which they had fulfilled faithfully for centuries, have been cruelly usurped by the male-only hierarchy. The 'constant' practice of the Church cited by John Paul II and other members of the hierarchy is a source of great shame. Furthermore, it is an unconscionable perversion of truth.

Sally Moran

PART III

MAGISTERIUM

Sally Moran

INTRODUCTION

The Doctrines They Teach Are Only Human Regulations

Is. 29:13

Magisterium is the term used to indicate the teaching authority claimed by the Roman Catholic Church. The Church believes that the Magisterium, its teaching mission, was instituted by Christ after His resurrection when He instructed the eleven Apostles to "Go and teach". (Similar to His mandate to Mary of Magdala, "Go and tell.") All four Gospels and the Acts of the Apostles relate a mission incident. The stories vary somewhat. Mark[1] describes the situation where the eleven were at table. Jesus reproached them for their obstinacy and failure to believe Mary of Magdala and the other women who had been at the tomb on Easter. Matthew[2] sets his incident on a mountain in Galilee where the eleven met Jesus. Some of the eleven hesitated to fall down before Jesus, indicative of lack of faith. Luke[3] describes the scene where the eleven, with their companions, some of whom were female, were gathered together when Jesus appeared in their midst. After teaching them about Scriptures, Jesus took them to the outskirts of Bethany, in Judea, where He blessed them and was carried 'up to heaven'. John places his version in the room where the disciples were assembled but Thomas was missing. John quotes Jesus, "As the Father sent me, so am I sending you"[4] The Acts of the Apostles, a continuation of Luke's Gospel, relates that Jesus told the group that they would be witnesses to the ends of the earth. Then He was lifted up and a cloud hid Him from their sight.[5]

Despite the variations in their telling, the gospel-writers agree on the scope of the mission: evangelize the entire world, preach to all nations, even to the ends of the earth. Based upon this Scriptural mandate, the Church maintains that it is commissioned by God to teach the truth. Truth in teaching is explained as that which is manifested by universal consent among all the bishops to the last of the faithful. Such general consensus is called 'sensus fidei'.

Unfortunately, development of such universal consent is, and frequently has been, hampered by the suppression of the findings of theologians, Biblical or Papal Commissions, and by punitive actions against dissenters and those called heretic. The Church believes that the guidance of the Holy Spirit preserves the Magisterium from error.

According to the documents of Vatican II, Scripture, Tradition and Magisterium are so interrelated and associated that one cannot stand without the other. Furthermore, the Magisterium depends upon theological interpretation of Scripture, Tradition, Contemporary Experience and Science in search for truth. Extraordinary Magisterium, also called Solemn Magisterium, consists of announcements from general councils, bishop's letters, patristic writing, doctrinal definitions and papal declarations relating to faith and morals. The term, Ordinary Magisterium, represents the continuous teaching which exists throughout the Church, for example, in homilies, lectures presented in houses of worship or prayer, in educational facilities, in the writings of saints and mystics, books, pamphlets and teaching programs. The Catechism[6] states that all of the faithful share in understanding and handing on of revealed truth since all have received anointing of the Holy Spirit. Therefore, it follows that all of the faithful, without gender limitation, participate in the genesis and development of Tradition and Magisterium.

Certain aspects of the Magisterium were codified into Canon Law. From the fourth century onward multiple laws were passed. Among the earliest codes were the Laws of Constantine (315 AD), the Laws of Constaninus (399 AD), the Laws of Theodosius II (439 AD) and the Laws of Justinian (531 AD). For centuries Church Law and Civil/State Law were one. Popes, Emperors or Kings held jurisdiction over matters of faith, convened councils, declared orthodoxy, punished heresy. In the first half of the twelfth century, Gratian, probably a monk, most likely a teacher of Law at Bologna, most certainly a scholar, set out to collect and organize the accumulation of Papal letters, laws, canons and texts extant. Completed by 1140 AD, the Decretum, once entitled the "Harmony of Discordant Canons," became the basis for Western Ecclesiastic Law. In 1230 AD, Raymond of Penyafort edited and codified Canons of the Church, including the Decreta. In 1231 AD, Pope Gregory IX issued a Bull declaring Raymond's work as authoritative. In 1578 AD, Pope Gregory XIII appointed a commission to edit the Decretum. In 1582 AD, this Pope authorized the edited version as the standard for Roman Catholics.

Until 1916, this Code of Law remained the chief source for legal guidance for canonists within the Roman Catholic Church. A major revision of Canon Law was completed in 1917 and again in 1983. Unfortunately for women and Jews, the Canon Law legitimized prejudice and repression.

The Vatican cites the Magisterium as if it were an unchanging entity. John Paul II, in his Apostolic Letter on Reserving Priestly Ordination to Men Alone, claims that the teaching "has been preserved by the constant and universal Tradition of the Church and firmly taught by the Magisterium."[7]   But, like Tradition, the Magisterium has not been constant in much of its teaching. For over twelve hundred years women were ordained to various ecclesiastic offices within the Church. It is difficult to believe that a Tradition which lasted for twelve centuries could have been at odds with the Magisterium. Ancient Church documents refer to such practices. Originally approved, eventually banned, one can trace the changes in Magisterium relative to the ordination of females.

Change has occurred in many other areas of the Magisterium including but not limited to: anti-Semitism, censorship, clerical celibacy, ecumenism, evolution, liturgical ritual, heresy, science, slavery, usury. Throughout history the pronouncements of Popes, Bishops, Councils (the Solemn Magisterium) contradict or nullify one another.

Invoking the concept of a constant practice to justify denial of ordination to females is illogical, even if such practice had indeed been constant. But, in the absence of such practice, the justification becomes ludicrous. Clearly, the constant practice claimed by the Vatican is a most serious misrepresentation of the truth.

Neither Tradition nor Magisterium has been constant throughout the ages.

POWER OF THE KEYS

In response to Jesus' query, "Who do you say I am?", Simon replied, "You are the Messiah, the Son of the Living God."[1] Matthew, Mark and Luke all relate Peter's acknowledgement of Christ's Messiah-hood. In all three gospels, following Peter's statement, Jesus strictly charged the disciples to tell no one of His identity. Only Matthew, previous to the order for secrecy, develops the incident. Jesus called Simon 'Peter', (Greek: Petros; Aramaic: Kepha) meaning rock, to indicate the foundation upon which the Church would rest. Jesus conferred on Peter 'the keys of the kingdom'. "Whatever you bind on earth shall be considered bound in heaven; whatever you loose on earth shall be considered loose in Heaven."[2]

The Church maintains that Simon's profession of Jesus' identity and mission forms the basis for his primacy among the Apostles.[3] This 'power of the keys' gave Peter authority to lead the Church. The Church teaches that Christ, by telling the Eleven that He would be with them "always; yes, to the end of time"[4] conferred the power of the keys not only upon Peter, but upon all of his successors. This power of the keys gives popes authority to lead the Church. The power to 'bind and loose' grants authority to absolve sins, pronounce doctrinal judgments and to invoke discipline within the Church.[5] Contrary to the Vatican's claims, Jesus' commission to Peter certainly connotes papal ability to include (actually to reinstate) women in ordained sacerdotal ministry.

After the resurrection, Jesus visited the disciples several times. John[6] relates the story where Jesus, on the shores of the Sea of Tiberius, cooked fish for John, Peter, Thomas, Nathaniel, Zebedee's sons and two other unnamed disciples (perhaps female?). In this scene Jesus asked Peter three times, "Do you love me?" And each time, after Peter professed his love for Jesus, he was instructed to, "Feed my lambs," "Tend me sheep," "Feed my sheep." Jesus never differentiated between ewes (female sheep) and rams (male sheep). Jesus never exhibited gender bias. And in the earliest days of

Christianity, there was no gender bias. The community of believers was of one heart and one mind.[7]

The 'keys of the kingdom' eventually became symbolic of Papal authority, appearing on the Papal Coat of Arms and Papal documents. This power of the keys which represents the initiation of the Magisterium "has been entrusted to the bishops in communion with the successor of Peter, the Bishop of Rome" according to the catechism of the Catholic Church.[8] From earliest times, the teachings of the bishops were intrinsic to the Magisterium.

The initial challenge to the teaching of Peter occurred quite early in Church history. As usual, conflict arose between two groups of Christians differing in culture and practice. The Christian Jews in Jerusalem clung to the 'Old Law' including circumcision and ritual uncleanness. Jesus had gone to great lengths to eradicate the concept of 'unclean' since this concept extended not only to pagans but to women. According to the Law, Jewish persons could not eat with pagans because they were not circumcised, hence they and their food were considered to be unclean. Also, according to the Law, pagans were not of the Chosen People. Peter had been visiting converted pagans and eating with them. When he returned to Jerusalem, some of the apostles criticized Peter, saying, "So, you have been visiting the uncircumcised and eating with them, have you?" It is quite possible that the Jewish Christians were referring to eating of the Ritual Meal (Eucharist). Peter, the first Bishop of Rome (although this title had not been devised as yet) was challenged by the Jewish Christians. According to Paul, Peter had been intimidated by friends of James because they had insisted upon circumcision for all converts. Even Barnabas bowed to the pressure. The 'old guard' wanted to keep the Jewish status quo. So Paul, who worked among the pagans, went to meet Peter, who had traveled to Antioch. Paul challenged Peter and opposed him to his face because Paul believed that Peter "was manifestly in the wrong."

Peter is symbolic of the 'old Traditional' ways. Peter, constrained by conservatives, still leaned towards the concept that Jesus, and Christianity, came only to the "lost sheep of the House of Israel."[9] Under Peter's guidance, much of the Old Law would still have been in practice, with its restrictive tendencies and its exclusion of Gentiles.

Paul is symbolic of the evolving Way. Paul converted pagans, worked with females who were deacons, disciples, leaders of prayer, teachers, prophets. He worked with a female apostle.

Peter is one of the original Eleven. Paul is a successor of that vacant twelfth place symbolic of other apostles, ie Mary of Magdala, Paul, Junia, Patrick, Cyril, Xavier, etc.

When the Vatican cites a constant Magisterium as justification for a teaching or a practice, it fails to remember that constancy did not exist even among the Eleven. From earliest Christianity, there were conflicting interpretations of the Word and contradictory teachings.

Peter's meeting with Paul set the stage for one method for resolving conflict. It represents the initiation of the 'council' as an instrument for the doctrinal, teaching, peacemaking and punitive functions within the Church. But early bishops believed that a council resolution needed unanimity. At the first council, held in Jerusalem in 52 AD, the apostles and other representatives of the Christian communities perceived unanimity to be a sign that the Holy Spirit approved of the proceedings. Following the deaths of the original apostles, disciples and Paul, the early Church began to adopt the customs of the Romans. The initial hierarchical structure was similar to that of the Roman army. And eventually Church Councils resembled proceedings of the Roman Senate (known as the Curia). Like Roman senators, the bishops gathered in semi-circular fashion. However, whereas a Senate resolution carried over to enactment with a majority vote (usually one more than half), the Church depended upon total agreement in order to promulgate any decision. The belief in unanimity, carried since 52 AD, heralded repressive and dangerous tactics.

In the second and third centuries, as persecution of the Christians waned (starting with Peter, eight successive bishops of Rome had been martyred by 136 AD) the bishops sought to bring stability to a rapidly growing Church. Utilizing the concept of Apostolic Succession,[10] they denounced dissenters, pronouncing them heretics. An early heresy was that of Gnosticism, which preached salvation through occult knowledge. It included elements of Jewish and

Hellenistic mysticism, Zoroastrianism, Babylonian and Egyptian mythology. The Montanist heresy denied forgiveness from sin and set up its own hierarchy. Tertullian, a respected Roman theologian and formidable defender of the faith, eventually left the Roman Church and became a Montanist. Manichaeism, a Persian synthesis of Gnostic, Buddhist, Taoist and Christian principles flourished in the third century. Donatus, bishop of Carthage, began a schism in Africa which lasted for three hundred years. But the influence of these sects paled in comparison with the Arian heresy of the fourth century.

Arius, a Christian priest from Alexandria, taught (c 318 AD) that Jesus was not equal to, nor coeternal with the Father. One doubts that the farmer plowing the field, the artisan working in the shop, the mercenary soldier, the camel-driver or the weaver pulling the flax was overly concerned with the intricacies of an inexplicable mystery. Yet Gibbon[11] claims that the unhappy discord disturbed the triumph of Constantine. And so the Emperor convoked the Council of Nice. Here he approved the Nicene Creed and declared that anyone who resisted the 'divine judgment' of the synod would be exiled. In the fourth century, an Emperor, head of a civil state, not ordained, perhaps still not baptized[12] convened a council, punished dissenters and contributed an essential element of the Extraordinary (Solemn) Magisterium. Arius was banished, his writings burned, his followers threatened with death. But within three years, the exiles were recalled and Arius was once again treated with respect. The Synod of Jerusalem[13] approved his faith, and Athanasius, who had previously championed orthodoxy against Arius, was deposed and banished. Another bishop, Gregory, was installed in his place. Athanasius then spent three years in exile, but was cleared subsequently by yet another council of fifty bishops in Italy.[14] In less than a decade, the 'constant' Solemn Magisterium, the teaching power of the Church, vacillated, reversed and contradicted its own dicta.

Soon afterward, two bishops, John Chrysostom (347-407 AD) and Augustine (354-430 AD) held widely divergent opinions on the manner of keeping the faithful free from heresy.

John Chrysostom was Patriarch of Constantinople. He was renowned, loved and respected for his eloquence, ascetic life and charity. John urged great effort, perseverance and patience in leading dissenters to the truth. He taught that persons must be led by persuasion, never by fear or force. John was a Father of the Greek Church.

Augustine was Bishop of Hippo, Algeria, a city, conquered by Rome around 100 B.C. He had spent his youth hedonistically, had fathered an illegitimate son and had adhered to the heresy of Manicheism. In Milan, at age thirty-three, he was baptized by Ambrose, Bishop of Milan. He returned to Hippo, became a priest and, eventually, a bishop. Due to the scope of his writings and his teachings, Augustine is viewed as co-founder, with Paul, of Western theology. A Father of the Latin Church, he initially praised the use of persuasion in dealing with dissenters, but later turned to coercion. He resorted to Roman civil tactics: fines, evictions, exile. He even utilized military force.[15]

Two bishops, each a 'Father' of the Church, each later canonized as a saint, demonstrate through their teaching concerning dissenters, a Magisterium at odds with itself.

Christianity initially seeded itself in the nations surrounding the Mediterranean Sea where the ruling monarchs devoutly adhered to the religions of the state. Some of them were considered to be divine while others acted as heads of the religion. As such they officiated at religious ceremonies and festivals. When Christianity gained stature, it was no longer considered a sect for the poor and uneducated. Members of the hierarchy were appointed by rulers or elected by citizens. They were selected from among the well educated, wealthy, powerful men who interacted with reigning monarchs. By the fourth century following the death of Christ, more than eighteen hundred bishops administered the Church. But synods and church councils (sources for the Extraordinary Magisterium) were convoked by emperors, empresses, kings or other civil authority. The reigning monarchs attended and frequently controlled the meetings. Members of the clergy who dared to disagree with civil interpretations of theological matters were exiled or executed by order of the monarch. Disagreements among members of the hierarchy (frequently reflecting regal opinions) were so encompassing that Hilary, Bishop of Poitiers (315-367 AD), decried the situation. "There are as many creeds as opinions, as many doctrines as inclinations. Every year, nay, every moon, we make new creeds."[16]   Hardly an example of a 'constant magisterium.'

Although there were bishops who practiced the charity of John Chrysostom, the Magisterium of the Latin Church continued to implement Augustinian tactics against dissenters, The freedom heralded by Paul was seriously curtailed.

That lost freedom has yet to be restored.

FREEDOM LOST

For the first two centuries, freedom was a primary message of the Church. Freedom from the repressive Old Law was cited by Paul, "Now we are rid of the Law, free to serve in a new spiritual way."[1] The Christians hailed freedom from segregation, living a classless society, following Paul's philosophy that there was no longer slave or free person, no male or female. All were one in Christ. The Church extolled freedom from emotional ties to the world through celibacy and monasticism. There was an awareness of freedom to choose good over evil.

But the subsequent strengthening of the hierarchy, the introduction of the concept of heresy with its expulsion of dissenters, seriously curtailed freedom of expression.

As far back as the second century, bishops had claimed the doctrine of Apostolic Succession. Clement, Bishop of Rome from 88 to 97 AD, who, according to Irenaeus (c 125-c 202 AD) had seen and conversed with the Apostles, in his Epistle to the Corinthians, expressed the belief that the Apostles had provided for others to carry on their ministry. Unfortunately for many, this ministry was seen by the bishops as belonging solely to them. All Christians were expected to obey the hierarchy. Irenaeus taught, "She (the Church) is the entrance to life; all others are thieves and robbers."[2] Ignatius, Bishop of Antioch asserted that, "Apart from the Church hierarchy there is nothing that can be called a church."[3] The hierarchy claimed exclusive rights to the truth. Dissenters were expelled from the community, labeled 'heretic'. Heresy was indeed considered to be more than merely sinful. It was perceived to be a threat to faith and was aggressively attacked throughout the ages. An old Canon directed that the Church should take care of the salvation of others by separating the heretic from the Church through excommunication and deliver the person to the secular court to be removed from this world by death. Saints Augustine (354-430 A.D.), Isadore (560-636 A.D.), Jerome (340-420 A.D.) and Thomas Aquinas (1225-1 274 A.D.) were among the supporters of death as punishment for heretics.

Throughout the centuries the Church continued to attempt to extinguish heresy. By the twelfth century the Church had instructed the civil authorities to prosecute heretics under the label 'anathema' one who was excommunicated (Second Lateran Council 1139 under Innocent III). This punishment was expanded by Alexander III (Pope 1162-1163 A.D.) to include confiscation of property. By 1229, Gregory IX, nephew of Innocent III, issued the Bull 'Excommunicamus" which mandated life imprisonment for a repentant heretic and death for an unrepentant heretic.

In 1233 A.D.[4] the Papal Bull 'Ille Humani Generis" instituted the Inquisition. Originally limited to Germany, it was extended throughout Aragon, France, Italy and Lombardy by 1237 A.D. The Dominicans were the chief Inquisitors. By 1254 A.D., those accused by the Inquisitors had no right to counsel, could not know the identity of their accusers, nor the charges levied against them. Among those accused of heresy were Ignatius Loyala (1491-1556 A.D.) founder of the Society of Jesus (known as the Jesuits) and Teresa of Avila (1515-1582 A.D.), reformer of the Carmelites, later a Doctor of the Church. Jeanne d'Arc, convicted of heresy, was burned at the stake in 1431 A.D.

In 1478 A.D., Sixtus IV (Pope 1471-1484 A.D.) issued a Bull which approved the Spanish Inquisition. This infamous Inquisition, initiated by Ferdinand and Isabel, was under the control of the Crown rather than of the Papacy, and indulged in vindictive extremes throughout the kingdoms of Spain. Punishment was so barbaric that in some cases posthumous condemnations occurred, involving exhumation of the remains of the convicted person so that such remains could be burned.

Repressive tactics in coping with actual or potential heresy continued throughout the centuries. Leo (Pope 1513-1521 A.D.) condemned Martin Luther in his Bull, 'Exsurge Domine'. Still reacting to the shock of the Reformation, Pius V (Pope 1566-1572 A.D.) established the Congregation of the Index (Index Librorum Prohibitorium), a list of books which Catholics were forbidden to read. The penalties for reading from this list included excommunication. The Index included such authors of diverse and highly respectable writings as Milton, Descartes, DeFoe, Maimonides,

John Chrysostom (a Doctor of the Church), Cyprian. The Book of Common Prayer and 'unauthorized' translations of the New Testament were also included. The Index was maintained under the Congregation of the Holy Office, originally the tribunal of the Roman Inquisition. The Vatican maintained and revised the index for four centuries, publishing the last Index in 1948. In 1965, Paul VI (Pope 1963-1978) abolished the Index and in 1966, the Congregation for the Doctrine of Faith (formerly the Congregation of the Holy Office (Roman Inquisition) announced that the penalties of excommunication related to the Index would no longer be considered lawful within the Church.

Too many of Peter's successors were wealthy, powerful, politically ambitious autocrats who consistently struggled with civil rulers for economic, military, geographic and spiritual control of the populace. For centuries, emperors, empresses, kings convoked councils and synods, while popes waged wars, called for crusades, mandated censorship. The Magisterium, under certain hierarchical members, was a source of abuse, intolerance, despotism and death. Frequently many of their pronouncements were eventually nullified, negating the concept of a 'constant' Magisterium.

Paul's joyous exclamation, "Now we are rid of the Law, free to serve in a new spiritual way" has been seriously hampered by an authoritarian, inconsistent Magisterium.

EUCHARIST

Rome, through the Magisterium, teaches that the Eucharist is the source and summit of Christian life,[1] the visible expression of the Church,[2] the sum and substance of the Roman Catholic Christian faith. As with other aspects of the Magisterium, teaching regarding Eucharist evolved throughout the centuries. There were innovations, abuses, revisions, additions, deletions. However, the essence - the Sacred Meal - began with Jesus at His Seder Meal during his last Passover Festival. During the first century after the ascension of Christ, the Christians shared the Sacred Meal within the early Home Churches. But shortly after the Apostolic Era, there was dissension within the Magisterium concerning the Liturgy. Ignatius, Bishop of Antioch (d 107 AD) taught that, "It is not legitimate to baptize or hold an agape (the ancient term for the Sacred Meal) without a bishop."[3] And in concert with this teaching Eucharistic liturgies moved into large edifices usually based in a city under the rule of the bishop. In Home Churches, the Sacred Meal had been conducted by deaconesses or deacons. In previous practice, deacons and deaconesses baptized. In current practice, baptism, the sacrament of Christian initiation, may be administered by a lay person of either gender, as well as by an ordained deacon, priest or bishop. Currently, the Eucharistic Liturgy is only rarely celebrated in the presence of a bishop.

By the fourth century, the cathedrals (churches which were the seat of an episcopal see) of Constantinople and Carthage maintained permanent establishments of approximately five hundred ecclesiastical ministers. This coterie included sixty priests, one hundred deacons, forty deaconesses, ninety sub-deacons, one hundred-ten readers (lectors), twenty-five chanters (cantors), one hundred doorkeepers (porters or portresses).[4] During the tenure of Gregory the Great (590-604 A.D.), the celebration of the Mass exceeded three hours. During the following years many differing rites of celebration of Eucharist developed, including Armenian, Byzantine, Celtic, Chaldean, Coptic, Greek, Milanese, Roman and Syrian. It is presumed each rite was in the vernacular, although Greek had yielded to Latin as the predominant language of the Church. As has been noted previously, the Magisterium, both the Solemn and Ordinary, was influenced, and in some areas, controlled, by civil authority. For example, Charlemagne overrode the objections of Leo III (Pope 795-816 A.D.) and mandated inclusion of the Nicene Creed within the liturgy celebrated in his domain. Centuries later, Henry II, in 1014 A.D., overrode the objections of Benedict VIII (Pope 1012-1024 A.D.) by including the Nicene Creed in the Roman Liturgy.[5]

From approximately 1200 A.D. to 1400 A.D., the Liturgy was a rite which had little importance for most of the laity. Religious dramas, parades and processions, pageants, novenas to saints, devotion to relics and icons, veneration of shrines were more popular with the laity than was attendance at Mass. Reception of the Eucharist under both species(bread and wine) disappeared. The Council of Constance (1414-1418 A.D.) prescribed reception of the Consecrated Bread alone. Frequent reception of Communion declined, especially among the laity. A poor Christian might live an entire lifetime receiving Communion only once as Viaticum (at one's death).[6] Such practice certainly demonstrated failure to obey Christ's directive, "Feed my sheep." The wealthy, however, maintained private chapels and live-in chaplains within their estates or manor houses, affording easy access to Eucharist.

In the sixteenth century, the Vatican reacted to the Protestant Reformation by promulgating the Latin (Tridentine: Latin for Trent) Mass. The Mass in any vernacular was banned, while the Roman Latin Mass was deemed universal. By order of Pius V (Pope 1566-1572 A.D.), anyone who deviated from the Latin Mass was anathema (excommunicated). The Roman Latin Mass was ordered "forever", in "perpetuity". In mandating the Roman Latin Mass, Plus V said that the rites "Were to be restored to the vigor which they had in the days of the Holy Fathers." Almost four hundred years later, those same words were used to enact revision of the Liturgy during Vatican II. In 1963 John XXIII convoked the Second Vatican Council (now commonly known as Vatican II). The Roman Latin Mass was no longer mandated. The Liturgical Reforms returned the Sacred Meal to the vernacular and increased the participation of the laity. Reception of Communion under both species was reinstated and the rules relating to preparation for reception of Communion were modified.

Among the many pronouncements of Vatican II was the Constitution of the Sacred Liturgy, which stated:

> The Sacred Council has set out to impart an ever increasing vigor to the Christian life of the faithful.[7]

Once again the Solemn Magisterium had changed its position and rightfully so. The reforms begun in Vatican II are still in development. In order that all of the faithful experience 'an ever increasing vigor', exhaustive Scriptural and theological research must occur so that ordained females, (disciples and apostles of Jesus), may experience Emmaus,[8] 'fractio panis': breaking of the Bread.

ANTI-SEMITISM

The International Theological Commission Study, approved in December 1999 by Joseph Cardinal Ratzinger, Prefect of the Congregation for the Doctrine of Faith, states "the history of the relations between Jews and Christians is a tormented one…" The use of the word 'tormented' is painfully appropriate.

It is so easy to forget that the earliest Christians were Jewish persons. The original Apostles, both female and male, were Jewish. The Roman citizen, Paul, was of the Jewish tribe of Benjamin, son of Rachel. But when Paul evangelized among the Gentiles, they then became the majority within the Christian Church. As early as the second century, some church leaders started to disparage Judaism. The 'torment' had begun. The Gospel of John, most likely written circa 95-115 A.D., describes the disciples as locked in a room "for fear of the Jews."[1] The disciples might have been in fear of members of the Sanhedrin, the Jewish religious court. They might have had reason to fear Annais or Caiaphas, the chief priests, or feared the pharisees or the Sadducees, but not the collective 'Jews'.

But some writers see John's usage as a result of early conflict with fellow Jews,[2] demonstrating the sad fact that by the end of the first century, antipathy to Jews had reared its ugly head. The Epistle of Ignatius, Bishop of Antioch 115 A.D., states: "To profess Jesus Christ while continuing to follow Jewish custom is an absurdity."[3] By the fourth century, Augustine declared "the true image of the Hebrew is Judas Iscariot, who sells the Lord for silver."[4] His contemporary, John Chrysostom, called Jews "perfidious murderers of Christ"[5] In the sixth century the Justinian Code, a compilation of Church Law and doctrine, became Roman State Policy. It seriously limited Jewish freedoms, confiscating property and mandating capital punishment for several offenses. In the eleventh century, hundreds of Jews were slaughtered by the Christian armies during the First Crusade, in 1096 A.D. And in 1215 A.D., the Fourth Lateran Council mandated the wearing of distinctive clothing by Jews and Saracens (Muslims). Church Canon 68 forced Jews to wear a 'horned hat' to identify them as sons of the devil. By this time, Christendom had extended throughout Europe. The culture, unfortunately, depicted the Jew as evil, loathsome, guilty. Art, plays, legends, songs, even sermons, all vilified the Jew. Along with witches and wizards, they were fuel for the stake.

By the twelfth century, anti-Judaism flourished throughout Spain. Civil authorities sought to separate Jews from Christians. In some areas they were secluded in specific living quarters and forced to wear distinctive clothing. They were prevented from participating in trade in the local markets. Civil ordinances forbade Jewish mid-wives from ministering to Christian women and Christians were not allowed to maintain Jewish servants. The Catholic populace indulged in assaultive behavior, stoning the Juderia (Jewish ghetto), invading and desecrating synagogues. Not only did the Church hierarchy do little to discourage such behavior, but the Magisterium actually fostered anti-Semitism. Alvara Perez, Bishop of Silves in Portugal (circa 1536 A.D.), said, "The perfidious Jews devour the bodies and possessions of the kings of Spain."[6] The Dominican, Vincent Ferrar (1350-1419 A. D.) said, "Just as prostitutes live apart, so should Jews."[7] The Archdeacon Martinez, avid anti-Semite, led a raid on Jewish quarters in 1391 A.D.

In March 1492 A.D., the edict expelling Jews from the kingdoms of Castile and Aragon was issued. Losing their homes, their possessions, subject to attack from thieves, tens of thousands of Jewish persons left Spain under horrific conditions. Generally, Christians applauded the grim fiasco. Alexander VI (Pope 1492-1503 A.D.), enthusiastically supported the Spanish monarchy's expulsion of the Jewish people from Spain...so much so that he believed that their actions had earned the title, "Catholic Monarch."[8]

In 1536 A.D. John Frederick of Saxony expelled the Jews from his electorate. In 1542 A.D. Paul III (Pope 1534-1549 A.D.) assigned the Congregation of the Inquisition to the Holy Office where it became known as the Roman Inquisition. It is worth noting that this same body of ecclesiastics convicted Galileo of heresy and condemned him to spend the rest of his life under house arrest. His heresy? Alleging that the earth revolved around the sun.[9] The Roman Inquisition, under Paul IV (Pope 1559-1565 A.D.), inflicted torture upon the Jews. Paul IV continued the Spanish practice of separating them into ghettoes, limiting their economic ability and forcing them to wear distinctive clothing. In fact, Roman Jews were forced to live in the ghetto until the twentieth century, until World War II.

Near the end of the fifteenth century, Jews had been expelled from Spain, Portugal, England and France. The Reformation did nothing to help the Jew. Luther's anti-Semitic writing echoed the repressive policy of the Roman Magisterium. Luther's philosophy?

> First, their synagogues should be burned down...their houses destroyed...their prayer books should be taken from them...rabbis forbidden to teach...away with them at all costs
> 10

Not until the nineteenth century, as a result of the social and civil changes following the Enlightenment, were Jews allowed to become true citizens of the European nations within which they lived. But this freedom was illusory. The late nineteenth century witnessed the widespread and deliberate slaughter of Jews in Eastern Europe. And in 1936 A.D., Polish Josef Cardinal Glamp said in a pastoral letter, "There will be a Jewish problem as long as the Jews remain." Within a few years, six million Jews, along with gypsies, the aged and the infirm, were murdered under the rule of the Nazis, while all too many 'Christians' remained silent.

How does one portray six million persons? Summon them forth. Call them: butchers, seamstresses, cobblers, bakers, teachers, charwomen, bankers, grandmothers, millers, widows, mothers, carpenters, doctors, school-children, toddlers, infants. Call them from the flower-filled lowlands of Holland, from the lace-making centers of Belgium, the vineyards of France. Ask them to congregate in New York City, near the eastern terminus of the George Washington Bridge. Ask them to line up side-by-side, shoulder-to-shoulder, facing north. Watch as their numbers fill the length of the bridge and stand alongside the garish, noisy Route 46 in New Jersey. Their line continues across New Jersey and they enter Pennsylvania at the Deleware Water Gap. Their line extends over the Pocono Mountains to Pittsburgh, across the Allegheny and Monangahela Rivers into Ohio. Call them forth from the Roman Ghetto, in the shadow of the

Vatican, and from the medieval villages of Poland. Ask them to line up, side-by-side, shoulder-to-shoulder, facing north. Watch as their line skirts south of Lake Erie passing Cleveland and Toledo through the neat farms of Amish country in Indiana, past South Bend into Illinois. Their silent line extends south of Chicago across the majestic Mississippi River. The column continues through the rolling landscapes of corn field in Iowa. Call them forth from the squeaky-clean hamlets of Germany. Watch them line up, side-by-side, shoulder-to-shoulder, facing north. See the human chain continue across the Missouri River into Nebraska, follow the course of the Platte River, through the Great Plains. See their line continue through spreading acres of wheat. They extend southwest into Colorado, a land of soaring mountains. Watch as the line ceases just short of Denver, the 'mile-high' city.

Now, like an eagle, fly high, soar above the shadowy wraith-like people, who, one by one, side-by-side, shoulder-to-shoulder, facing north, stretch from Denver to New York City, just slightly more than two thousand miles. That's the six million persons exterminated by the Nazis without any cry of shame or fraternal fury from most of Christianity. For as late as 1945 A.D., while Jews languished, suffered and died in Auschwitz, Dachau and other segments of Hell, Roman Catholics prayed during their Solemn Liturgy on Good Friday as follows: "Almighty and eternal God who drivest not away from Thy mercy, even the faithless Jews..."[11]

Thankfully, however, John XXIII (Pope 1958-1963 A.D.), through his life and teachings, reversed the anti-Semitic stance of the Magisterium. During World War II, he had assisted many Jews to emigrate through Turkey, thus escaping the Nazis. As Pope, he ordered deletion of the term "perfidious Judaeis"(faithless Jews) from the Liturgy. Vatican II, convoked by John XXIII, on "Nostra Aetate", October 28, 1965, recalled the words of the Jewish Apostle Paul concerning the Jewish people, "They are the Israelites, and to them belong the sonship, the glory, the Covenants, the giving of the Law, the worship and the promises..."[12] Furthermore, Nostra Aetate condemned any discrimination based on race, color, condition of life or religion (note yet again, the absence of gender). After the passage of many centuries, the Solemn Magisterium began to correct the shameful errors of the past. The unchanging 'constant' Magisterium, thankfully, had changed yet again.

In March 2000, for the first time in two thousand years, an incumbent Pope made an official visit to Israel, now a Jewish nation. John Paul II, a Pole, had been accused of being 'passive' during the Holocaust, not unlike the charge against Pius XII.[13] Yet, John Paul II has made more overtures to the Jewish people than any previous pontiff. He visited Auschwitz, prayed in Synagogue. He led the Vatican to establish diplomatic relations with Israel in 1993. And, in 1998, he apologized for the silence of Catholics during the murder of millions in World War II. For many Jews, it is 'too little, too late'. However, for all of us, it is important.

John Paul's behavior, his writings, his lesson, is that two thousand years of Tradition, two thousand years of Solemn and Ordinary Magisterium are not immutable. If the Church can appear to change its position on so significant, long-standing, and tormented an issue as Judaism, then...it can and should change on another issue: the ordination of women.

SLAVERY

Like humanity's faith in supernatural beings, the origin of slavery antedates history. Geographically and culturally universal, slavery existed within the communities of seafaring Norsemen, among nomadic tribes of Europe, along the caravan routes which lead to Asia, and in Africa. It flourished in the urban centers of Persia, Egypt, Mesopotamia, in the lands surrounding the Mediterranean Sea and among the hunters of the Western Hemisphere. Whether living and working in the Asian steppes, in the African rain forests, or in the fertile lands of Europe, slaves were people bound to other persons as instruments of labor. They were sold into slavery in order to redeem debts, were bound into slavery as punishment for crimes or were captured and forced into subjection. Prisoners of war were routinely enslaved. Many of these prisoners were women and children, since soldiers (male) tended to be killed by their conquerors. In some near-eastern societies, males were enslaved, castrated and assigned to protect harems.

For millennia slaves had no rights. At the slave market husbands and wives were sold to different householders while children were enslaved separately from their parents. Their lives were at the disposal of their masters who exercised ultimate authority for discipline. Such discipline included branding with red-hot instruments, scourging and execution, frequently by crucifixion.

The price for a slave varied according to age, gender and health. For example, a male aged five to twenty years cost twenty shekels, a female of the same age, ten shekels. A male between twenty and sixty years of age was priced at fifty shekels, a like female at thirty.[1] Judas Iscariot sold Jesus for the price of a female slave, and Jesus was executed in the manner of a slave.

Within Judaism, the Patriarch Abraham, (c1800B.C.) included his male slaves in circumcision, affording them some spiritual identity.[2] According to Mosaic Law, Israelite slaves were freed after seven years' labor, but Gentile slaves had no hope for freedom.[3]

Hammurabi (1792-1750 A.D.), king of Babylonia, developed a code of civil law. Most likely influenced by Sumerian and Semitic

Law, the code, generally considered to be humanitarian, was harshly severe and punitive in reference to slaves. Plato (427-347 B.C.) described the slave as a semi-rational sub-human creature. Aristotle (384-322 B.C.) considered the slave to be merely a tool, only an animated piece of property. He believed that the slave had only limited reason and a slight capacity for friendship. Aristotle's concept of the ideal family unit included the master, his wife, children and slaves. Aristotle taught that the master should rule his slaves despotically, his wife, constitutionally, his children monarchically. Unfortunately for many, his writings influenced later leaders and theologians, many of whom were within the Church of Rome.

In contrast to all of this, Zeno of Cyprus (342-262 B.C.), founder of the Stoics, taught that all men were equal. And the Essenes, an Israelite sect, rejected all slavery as incompatible with the brotherhood of man.

The Roman slaves, like their counterparts in other societies, were integral to the economic, social and civic life of the community. Uncounted in the census (like women), they had no rights and were frequently subjected to cruelty. The Servile Wars, which were slave rebellions in 134-132 B.C., 104-101 B.C., and 73 B.C., were ruthlessly crushed by Rome's military forces. Some mitigation occurred under Hadrian, Emperor from 117 to 138 A.D., who allowed slaves to be tried in civil court rather than be executed by their masters.

Initially, the advent of Christianity heralded freedom, even for the slaves. James, the brother of the Lord, was quite specific in his teaching, "Do not try to combine faith in Jesus Christ with making of distinctions between people."[4] Peter taught, "You are slaves to no one except God, so behave like freemen...have respect for everyone...fear God and honor the emperor. Slaves must be respectful and obedient to their masters...even when they are unfair."[5] Such teaching was politically circumspect. Paul preached freedom from the Law.[6] But Paul's freedom was mostly limited to the spiritual laws of Judaism. For example, in Achaia, members of the Jewish community brought Paul before the proconsul, Gallio, charging Paul with breaking the Law. But Gallio gave them no satisfaction.[7] Such frequent harassment of Paul by members of the Sanhedrin demonstrated their concern for

Paul's religious teachings rather than socio-economic principles. Concerning slaves, Paul taught employers to treat their slaves without threats.[8] To the Colossians Paul told slaveholders to give to their slaves what was fair and just. Paul, in his letter to Philemon, returned the slave, Onesimus, to his rightful owner, offering to pay Philemon if the slave "has wronged you in any way". He asked Philemon to accept Onesimus as a brother. Paul demonstrated the Christian view of slavery: obey the law, but seek brotherhood with the slave, difficult to achieve, somewhat similar to Christ's injunction, "Give back to Caesar what belongs to Caesar and to God, what belongs to God."[9] But Paul also taught, "baptized in Christ, you have all clothed yourselves in Christ and there are no more distinctions between Jew and Greek, slave and free, male and female, but all of you are one in Christ."[10] Such teachings were reflected in the behavior of some Christians. The earliest Christians, residents of Jerusalem, described in Acts, lived together, owned all in common, went to the Temple together daily and met in their houses for the Breaking of the Bread. Wealthy Christians bought slaves in order to free them, while other Christians sold themselves into slavery and then used their purchase price to help the poor.[11] Apparently so many Christians participated in these practices that Ignatius (d 107 A.D.) in Epistle to Polycarp, discouraged the ransom of slaves at the expense of the community.

In early cenobitic monasticism, the concepts of equality and freedom, extolled by Paul and James, flourished. Slaves and free-persons lived in community with one another. But within other areas of the Christian community, slavery was considered to be such an essential part of human society that its abolition would cause grievous moral injury. Therefore, Christianity's Magisterium focussed on the spiritual welfare rather than the physical plight of enslaved persons. By 340 A.D., the Church Council of Gangra in Asia Minor mandated that anyone who taught a slave not to serve the master with good will and respect be declared anathema.[12] Circa 400 A.D., Augustine directed slaves to fulfill their faithful service to their masters in a Christian manner, i.e., with fear and trembling.[13] Augustine further interpreted slavery to reflect the Divine Order: sin is a primary cause of servitude. Ambrosiaster[14] wrote that masters had duties to their slaves and that because of evil, certain persons were rightfully reduced to servitude.

Thus the Magisterium, by accentuating the 'spiritual' plight of enslaved persons, left the morally reprehensible practice of slavery unscathed.

Meanwhile, the equality of persons within monasticism came under the attention of the hierarchy. The Council of Agde, held in 506 A.D., banned abbesses from depleting Church property by freeing slaves.

Gregory the Great (Pope 590-604 A.D.) taught that all men were created by God, but, as a consequence of sin, different classes of men had been produced. Isidore (c590-636 A.D.), Bishop of Seville, a Doctor of the Church, who presided at the Church Councils of Seville (619 A.D.) and Toledo (633 A.D.), utilized Aristotelian theory in his explanation that the behavior of those unfit for freedom must be controlled by those of a higher nature, the master. He wrote that slavery was part of God's providence. Isadore's theories were validated at the Council of Aachen (817 A.D.) thus becoming part of the Solemn Magisterium.

The advent of Islam in the sixth century complicated matters significantly. A major source of slaves had always been war, with conquered peoples routinely enslaved by their victors. Conflicts of a religious nature added frenzy to an already horrific activity. When the Islamic Caliph Umar conquered Jerusalem in the seventh century, the followers of Allah occupied Christendom's holiest sites, causing inevitable skirmishes. By the eleventh century, the Caliph Hakin had persecuted Christian pilgrims and desecrated the holy places. So the next three centuries were subject to chronic warfare. The Crusades against the Muslims, combined with the battles against the Prussians, Slavs and Tartars in Europe, reduced many thousands to slavery.

Both Christianity and Islam utilized the concept of a 'just war' to enslave people. The Qu'ran permitted prisoners of war to be held in ransom until peace was achieved. Infidels were to be bound while in captivity. Both Islam and Christianity taught the 'justice' of the enslavement of infidels. Rome taught that slavery was a morally acceptable state for those captured during war.

Yet there were other members of the hierarchy who denounced slavery. In 1102 A.D., the Synod of London forbade any further traffic in slaves. "Let no one hereafter presume to engage in that nefarious trade in which hitherto in England men were sold like brute animals."[15]

The Age of Exploration pushed the boundaries of slavery ever further. Portugal trafficked in African slaves, Spain in Native Americans. Alexander VI (Pope 1492-1503 A.D.) granted full permission to capture and subjugate pagans and other unbelievers as the enemies of Christ. Hence, by invoking religion, the Church of Rome justified the systemic enslavement of countless persons with the dictum: convert or be captured. Bartolome de Las Casas (1474-1566 A.D.), a Spanish missionary priest, Bishop of Chiapa, actively tried to abolish slavery in the Western Hemisphere. But, Paul III (Pope 1534-1549 A.D.) maintained the right of clergy and laity to own slaves.

In 1794, France decreed the abolition of slavery, and in 1807, England abolished the slave trade. But between 1579 and 1807 more than five million slaves had been imported into the New World. In 1839 Gregory XVI(Pope 1831-46 A.D.) declared: "Believers in Christ...no one may dare to molest Indians, Negroes or other men...or to reduce them to slavery."

On January 1, 1863, the American Emancipation Proclamation legally abolished slavery in the United States.

And more than a century later, in 1965, the Second Vatican Council stated:

> Whatever violates the integrity of the human person, such as mutilation, torture inflicted on body or mind, attempts to coerce the will itself; whatever insults human dignity, such as subhuman living conditions, arbitrary imprisonment, deportation, SLAVERY (emphasis mine)...all these things...poison human society, dis-honour the Creator...[16]

The Magisterium, both Solemn and Ordinary, has not been constant in its teaching concerning slavery. Like its treatment of other subjects, the Magisterium has reversed itself. Rather than function as

Sally Moran

a moral, spiritual leader, it has lagged behind the secular world in eliminating a most heinous practice.

WOMAN IN MAGISTERIUM

What is the teaching of Rome concerning women since the early years of the Church? It has been anything but consistent. For example, one can trace the inconstancy of the Magisterium concerning female deacons (deaconesses). In his letter to the Romans which was written about 58 A.D., Paul said, "I commend to you our sister, Phoebe, a deacon of the Church at Cenchreae. Give her, in union with the Lord, a welcome worthy of saints." In the year 300 A.D., the Syrian document, "Didascalia Apostolorum"[1] said, "The deaconess shall be honored by you in the place of the Holy Spirit." Note the similarity between Paul's "in union with the Lord" and "in the place of the Holy Spirit". Each statement evidences profound respect. Within a very short time, however, the Magisterium displayed confusion concerning the ordination of a female to the diaconate. Ambrose (340-397 A.D.), Archbishop of Milan, announced that women were not allowed to hold office in the Church,[2] while conversely, Ambrose's contemporary, Jerome, maintained that women held office in the Eastern Church, thereby justifying ordained office for females. However, during the same period, the Roman Emperor Theodosius (346-395 A.D.), ruled that only females over sixty years of age could be ordained while John Chrysostom ordained his friend and patron, the widow of Olympias, to the diaconate at the age of thirty. Then in 441 A.D., the Council of Orange, forbade the ordination of deaconesses. Later, the Synod of Nimes complained that women who claimed to be deaconesses invalidated the very concept of ordination. About this time, Ecclesiastic Law stated, "Let no one proceed to the ordination of deaconess anymore."[3] And in 533 A.D., the Council of Orleans stated, "No longer shall the blessing of women deaconesses be given because of the weakness of the sex.[4]

So, from the enthusiastic, respectful attitude of Paul, through the legalistic pique of civil authority, to the negativity of the Solemn Magisterium, one can readily see the destruction of the role of women in the ordained ministry of the diaconate.

And females suffered as apostles also. Paul, in his letter to the Romans, is worthy of note. He sends greetings to Junia, whom he calls his compatriot, fellow-prisoner, a Christian prior to his own conversion, and an OUTSTANDING APOSTLE. (emphasis mine) Much later the Patriarch, Doctor of the Church, John Chrysostom, (345-407 A.D.) said about Junia, "Indeed, how great the wisdom of this woman must have been that she was even deemed worthy of the title of apostle."[5] As mentioned previously, Aegidius of Rome in the thirteenth century changed her gender to male. Also, in the thirteenth century, the theologian, philosopher John Duns Scotus (1266-1308 A.D.), in considering the ordination of females to the priesthood, admitted that Mary of Magdala was indeed an apostle, a preacher, and an overseer of penitent women. However, he did not accept her apostleship as validation of female ordination. Even though the Magisterium teaches that the episcopacy was passed from the Apostles, Scotus interpreted Mary of Magdala's undisputed Apostleship as a 'personal privilege' granted to Mary by Jesus.[6] Rather than assessing such 'personal privilege' as an enhancement of Mary's apostolic role, Scotus used the concept to circumvent the Scriptural reality of female Apostolic Succession. Despite the acceptance of Scriptural support for female Apostleship by two noted men of the Church, the Vatican still insists that only males were chosen by Jesus for apostleship, thereby denying the fact of female Apostolic Succession with its incumbent priesthood.

Abbesses too were subject to the vagaries of the Magisterium. Further examples of an inconstant Magisterium may be seen in the rules governing the age at which a nun might become an abbess. Gregory the Great (Pope 590-604 A.D.) mandated that an abbess be at least sixty years old, noting that such an advanced age would be accompanied with discretion. Innocent IV (Pope 1243-1254 A.D.) and Boniface VIII (Pope 1294-1303 A.D.) changed the age to thirty. Then the Council of Trent (1545-1563 A.D.) directed that the abbess be at least forty years old.

And although Abbesses had enjoyed power, wealth, distinction, authority and ordination, bishops throughout history worked to subvert their position within the Church. In 1210 A.D., Pope Innocent III issued a letter which included this segment:

"Recently some news has come to our ears, which has caused no small amazement, namely that abbesses, resident in the dioceses of Burgos and Palencia (in Spain) bless their own nuns, hear their confession on crimes, and reading the Gospel, give public sermons. Since this is both incredible and absurd, and not to be tolerated by us, I am sending to your discretion, through these apostolic writings, the order to suppress this firmly with apostolic authority so that it does not happen again. For although the most blessed Virgin Mary was so much more worthy and excellent than all the Apostles, the Lord did not entrust to her, but to the Apostles, the keys of the kingdom of heaven."

Thus Mary's maternal role became a 'theological' basis for denial of priesthood to women. Because the Mother of Jesus was not an Apostle, all women were barred from ordination. This letter of Innocent III conveniently ignored the apostleship of Mary of Magdala and Junia. If one accepts the teaching that priesthood comes through apostleship, then women certainly qualify for ordination since Scripture, Tradition and the Magisterium identify at least two female apostles.

The Magisterium did not limit its maltreatment of females to women within ordained ministry. Basil the Great (330-379 A.D.), Bishop of Caesarea, warned women of their devastating effects upon men while John Chrysostom claimed that, "Women take all their corrupting feminine customs and stamp them into the souls of men."[7] Augustine and Ambrose also saw women as sources of temptation and sin. The Decretum of Gratian stated "Quia mulier est in statu subiectionis"[8] which translates as "woman is in a state of subjection." The Codex Iuris Canonici (Code of Canon Law) in force 1234-1916 A.D. described women as follows:

the word 'woman' signifies weakness of mind
in everything a wife is subject to her husband
woman is not created in the image of God
woman may not exercise liturgical office in church
woman may not teach in church

145

woman may not teach or baptize [9]

Thomas Aquinas echoed Gratian in his 'Summa Theologica' where he stated, "woman is naturally subject to man because in man the discernment of reason predominates."[10] This renowned theologian, Saint and Doctor of the Church further explains:

> It was necessary for woman to be made as helper...As regards the individual nature, woman is defective and misbegotten, for the active power in the male seed tends to the production of a perfect likeness according to the masculine sex; while the production of woman comes from a defect in the active power, or even from some external influence, such as that of a south wind which is moist...[11]

While this statement reflects the absolute ignorance of biology and genetics common to the century, unfortunately such ignorance is still reflected in Rome's position concerning women in the twenty-first century. Why this recurrent denunciation of persons of feminine gender? Does it revert to man's ancient fascination, with fear and concomitant taboo, of that uniquely female function-menstruation?

Male abhorrence of menstruation continued after the advent of Christianity. Dionysius of Alexandria (190-264 A.D.) banned all Christian women from entering the Church or participating in the Eucharistic Liturgy while they were menstruating. Gregory I, in the sixth century stated that a woman could not be barred from reception of communion during her menses, but that if she voluntarily refrained, she was worthy of praise. Eastern Orthodox churches banned menstruating females from attendance at Church. Canon Law proscribed women from reception of communion during their monthly periods until 1916. In sixteenth century France, women were banned from communion after childbirth until ritually purified. Remnants of such taboos still survive in cultures as diverse as the Maori of New Zealand and some sects of conservative monotheism. 'Churching,' a purification rite of women after childbirth, was still practiced in the Roman Catholic Church in the United States until the latter half of the twentieth century.

Hence, the Magisterium teaches that the very act of childbirth is considered, in some inexplicable way, to be suspect, unclean. Yet Rome still explains woman's role to be chiefly procreative, a role historically dirty...despite the example of Jesus. Although Jesus and Paul freed women from ritual uncleanness, Church Law encased women within spiritual as well as physical uncleanness for almost twenty centuries.

The Magisterium, throughout the ages, has reversed itself in many areas. Now, true to its history, the Magisterium seems to be starting to reverse its teaching concerning women, In the encyclical "Mulieris Dignitatum", (the dignity of woman), John Paul II states that "Man is a person, man and woman equally so, since both were created in the image of the personal God." This teaching is in direct conflict with Aquinas, and many others. Furthermore, equality between the genders recalls the freedom of the early Christians, a time when persons of either gender participated fully in Jesus' commission, "Go, tell...go, preach...feed my lambs...tend my sheep." Once the Magisterium fully professes equality between genders, the concept of a male-only priesthood is exposed for the indefensible position that it is.

John Paul II further states in his *Crossing the Threshold of Hope* that the 'position of women in life, not only family life, but also social and cultural life' is being redefined. Again John Paul II contradicts Aquinas and the Canon Law which held that women were created only to help man in regeneration of the species. Of course, one wonders about John Paul II's concept of social and cultural life when he quickly refers this redefinition to Mary, whose role was Motherhood of Jesus. Here again, the Magisterium lags behind the secular world where the roles of women have gone beyond definition to actual practice. Women by their accomplishments, have redefined themselves as capable of much more than motherhood. John Paul II further states that the "authentic theology of woman is being reborn."[12] One may infer from such a statement that the previous theology was insufficient, incomplete or erroneous. But when one contrasts the extreme misogynistic posture of the magisterium with the nearly idolatrous aspects of the Marian cult within the Roman Church, one questions the very existence of any authentic theology of woman in Catholicism.

147

Sally Moran

PART IV

Sally Moran

CONCLUSION

So the weary struggle continues...Peter versus Paul, conservative versus liberal, the Vatican versus the People of God. Certain members of the hierarchy still myopically maintain that Christ chose only men for pastoral leadership, refusing to consider the reality offered to them by theologians and Biblical exegetes. They claim the issue is doctrinal, hence, yet again, immutable. But just what is doctrine? And who decides it? Doctrine is one of those terms which so many persons 'know' but so few can define. Doctrine, from Latin doctrina meaning "to teach", is close to the Greek didaktikos meaning "skilled in teaching." Within the Church, doctrine is the imparting of knowledge from the deposit of faith in order to draw persons into closer union with God.[1] The term 'deposit of faith' refers to those teachings of truth revealed by Christ. His teaching includes that found in Old Testament Scripture. Additionally, teaching of truths contained in the books of the New Testament are considered as part of the deposit of faith. The Church maintains that revelation of the truth ended with the death of the last apostle. However, some elements of doctrine which were not explicit in the original deposit of faith have developed into dogmatic tradition.[2] Such elements are considered to have been implicitly revealed to the Church by God.

The Church invokes its claim to infallible authority in order to substantiate dogma. According to some writers, Christian doctrine cannot be proclaimed in isolation from human experience and thought.[3] "Whenever the Church is confronted with a new situation, there is a need to re-present the Christian teaching."[4] And like Tradition and Magisterium, doctrine develops. So using the term 'doctrinal' to buttress maintenance of a statusquo concerning ordination of females is merely obstructive, since Scripture (the essential source for the deposit of faith) does not forbid -but actually favors - ordination of women.

Joaquin Navarro-Valls, Vatican spokesman, reacting to the Church of England's ordination of thirty-two women to the priesthood in March 1994, explained that the Roman Catholic Church does not ordain women due to:

a) fidelity to the teaching of Jesus Christ[Magisterium]
b) uninterrupted practice throughout the centuries[Tradition]
c) theological reasons[Scripture]

These reasons are the same as those quoted by Paul VI and John Paul II.

The Vatican's contention that 'fidelity to the teachings of Christ' prohibits ordination of females displays an incredible lack of appreciation of Scripture and an arrogant rejection of females since Jesus' behavior and teaching did not endorse exclusion of females from any aspect of ministry.

History proves the Vatican's claim to 'uninterrupted practice' is simply not true. For centuries females were ordained and functioned in hierarchical offices within the Roman Catholic Church.

The term 'theological reasons' defies explanation, unless one accepts the misogynistic opinions of the likes of Aristotle and Aquinas, or the assertion of Innocent III. According to Leo XIII (Pope 1878-1902 A.D.), Holy Scripture is the soul of theology. Scripture not only fails to support exclusion of females from ordained ministry, Scripture actually supports the inclusion of women in every area of the life of Christ's Church. Theology, and many theologians, support the ordination of females. Throughout history, including the twentieth century, such theologians were silenced by Rome.

Despite the reforms initiated by Vatican II, too many members of the hierarchy have slammed shut the open windows of John XXIII, having lost the sight and the sense of the foundation and the mission of the Church, which is to live the Gospel, the Scripture.

"As soon as you make distinctions between classes of people you are committing sin," are the words of James, the 'brother of the Lord.'[5] Therefore, exclusion of women from ordained ministry constitutes spiritual violence and social aggression because it condones the subjugation of an entire gender.

According to the Catechism of the Catholic Church, the sacrament of Holy Orders, like Baptism and Confirmation, confers an indelible spiritual character.[6] The soul, which is the spiritual principle in a human person, is gender free. The Council of Vienne (1311-1312 A.D.), in contrast with Aquinas, determined that the soul is not in the form of a human body. Since Holy Orders is concerned with the spiritual, not the physical, element of a human, it follows that Holy Orders should not be gender limited. The Catechism also states that "since the beginning, the ordained ministry has been conferred and exercised in three degrees: bishop, presbyter and deacon.[7] As has been demonstrated in this work and elsewhere, in the beginning the three degrees, bishop (episkopa/episkopus), priest (presbytera/presbytero), and deacon (diakonos), were conferred on persons of either gender. Most unfortunately, reporting of the Tradition and of the history of the Magisterium of the Roman Catholic Church has been altered. Such alteration constitutes grievous manipulation of history to the spiritual detriment of countless persons, indeed, to the very soul of the Roman Catholic Church.

The history of humanity records a trans-cultural, eons old repression of females. Such repression resulted from fear, ignorance and superstition on the part of the males. But currently, and throughout civilization, women have demonstrated their ability to fulfill roles in the arts, sciences, business, politics and religion. Women have continued to function within organized religion filling the old customary roles while broadening their scope as barriers have fallen. Even within the Church of Rome, women have shrugged off much of the patriarchal encrustation of centuries. So rather than cling to an erroneous theologically indefensible posture regarding ordained ministry for women, the Vatican should reassess Scripture, re-study Tradition, listen to theologians, Biblical Commissions, correct the Magisterium. It is time to follow the advice of the renowned theologian, ostracized by Rome, Hans Kung, "We must not be silent...lack of courage can involve guilt."[8]

There are more than sixty million Roman Catholics in the United States. Approximately sixty-one percent of them favor ordination of women.[9] Included in that data are bishops, priests, lay persons and religious women and men. However, beyond the urgency of the majority of Catholics' desire for the ordination of women, lies a more compelling reason: need.

Throughout the United States, in the last decade, all dioceses were experiencing significant reduction in priests, from a 5% reduction in Los Angeles, CA. to a 31% reduction in Burlington, VT. Further declines are projected for the future,[10] and the decline of priests throughout the world is no secret. Within the last thirty years, the number of priests has declined by 40%. Conservative estimates for the next three to five years project the ratio of priests to the faithful will be one to two thousand (1:2000). An appalling situation…especially coupled with the fact that the average age of the priest will be sixty-four years.

Hundreds of Roman Catholic Churches have closed and more than two thousand five hundred parishes are priestless. Many of these parishes are led by pastoral administrators of the feminine gender who perform countless tasks, except anointing the sick, giving absolution for sins, and most essential, celebrating the Eucharist.[11] In 'priestless' parishes, persons of either gender may conduct 'communion service'. This ritual contains all of the parts of the Liturgy: penitentional rite, prayers, psalm response, Scripture readings, distribution of Communion, hymns, except for the actual consecration of the species, the sacrifice.

Throughout the centuries, mothers introduced little children to the existence of God and taught them to pray. Mothers fostered religious vocations. Although more than half of mothers now work outside the home many mothers still fulfill this role. But such women cannot continue to see, hear, read and experience the obvious contradiction between the spoken, written words and the actions of the institutional Church without pain and disillusionment.

John Paul II speaks of evangelization as an encounter with the culture of each epoch. Today's epoch is one which involves females in all roles in most institutions save within the Church of Rome. John Paul II has said,[12] "Those situations in which women are barred from developing their full potential and offering the richness of their gifts, are to be considered profoundly unjust." He has been quoted as saying 'real equality' for women remains an urgent goal.[13] But his statements are irreconcilable with his position concerning the ordination of females. In his book, *Crossing the Threshold of Hope,*[14] John Paul II says, "It is above all in the writing of Paul that one must search for the first expressions of the faith." Paul spoke of the priesthood as rising on the foundation of the apostles and prophets. But, there were female prophets in both the Old and New Testaments.[15] Paul spoke of female deacons, a female apostle, female martyrs, female leaders, female preachers in the Church. Why does John Paul II fail to read the message of Christ and Paul in Scripture? The chasm between Papal writings concerning women and John Paul II's decision to continue to prohibit their ordination is an enormous obstacle to the growth of the Spirit within the People of God, who are the Church. Without woman's continued faith and support the Church will suffer. In fact, such suffering has already begun. Currently, according to recent data, only twenty-seven percent of American Catholics attend Eucharist weekly. Furthermore, in a recent study sponsored by the National Conference of Catholic Bishops, it became evident that approximately twenty percent (20%) of Roman Catholic parents would strongly oppose a child's desire to become a priest or to enter religious life.

Meanwhile, blithely ignoring this situation, John Paul II recently prepared for the celebration of the new millennium. He directed Catholic Christians to use the few remaining years of the twentieth century as a 'New Advent' in celebration of Christ's birth.[15] Each year during the Advent Season, the prescribed Scriptural readings recount the stories relevant to the birth of Jesus. Ironically, these readings are particularly woman-centered. There is Mary of Nazareth, the young woman who birthed Jesus,[16] the barren Elizabeth who birthed John the Baptizer, and the aged prophet, Anna, who spoke of the Child to all. Finally, there are the women of Bethlehem and the surrounding areas who refused to be comforted for the loss of their sons.[17]

In the opening years of the third millennium since Jesus' birth, there are multitudes of women refusing to be comforted in their grief. Like the women of Bethlehem, they refuse to be consoled in their loss. Like Mary of Bethany, they have been called to a better part:[18] ordained ministry in the Roman Catholic Church, but in contempt for Jesus' mandate, it has been taken from them.

Vatican II set out to adapt "more closely to the needs of our age." The needs of our age include evangelization and vocations to the ordained priesthood. Our age should return women to the full role commissioned for them by Christ.

Paul, in his letter to the Romans,[19] described the Israelites as adopted children who were given the glory, the covenants, the Law, the ritual, the promises. From their flesh and blood came Christ. We Christians through Baptism are adopted children, who through Christ have glory and the New Covenant, have the new Law: love one another, preach, baptize. We, through Christ, have the new ritual: the Eucharist. Isn't it appropriate now, to function in a new millennium with a new, honest, humble hierarchical reform?

Is it too naive to expect a male-only clique to hear Sarah's injunction:

Listen, now!

Is it too naive to expect a male-only clique to remember that Jesus sent Mary of Magdala with the commission:

Go, tell the brethren.

EPILOGUE

Jesus Christ came by water and blood…there are three witnesses, the Spirit, the water and the blood.

1 John 5:6-7

REFERENCES/NOTES

Preface

1 International Theological Commission, December 1999 Vatican
2 John Paul II. *Ordinatio Sacerdotalis* L'Osservatore Romano N22 (1343) 1 June 1994, pg 2
3 Libreria Editrice Vaticana *Catechism of the Catholic Church* St. Paul Books and Media 1994 pg 493 #1782
4 Ratzinger, Joseph Cardinal, Prefect, Congregation for the Doctrine of Faith *National Catholic Reporter* Vol.34 Num.34 July 17. 1998 pp 18-19
5 Flannery, O.P., A. *Vatican Council II, The Conciliar and Post-Conciliar Documents.* Eerdman's Pub. Co., Grand Rapids, MI. 1992 pg 755
6 Ibid pg 754
7 Ibid pg 756
8 Bohlen, Celestine. *Pope Calls for an End to Discrimination Against Women* The New York Times, International, 11 July 1995 pg A11
9 Murphy, C. *Women and the Bible* The Atlantic Monthly, Vol. 272, Num.2 Aug. 1993 pg 43
10 Ostling, R. *Galileo and Other Faithful Scientists* Time, Vol. 140 Num. 26 pg 43
11 Chardin, S.J., T. *The Phenomenon of Man* Harper & Row, New York, N.Y. 1959 pg 234
12 Jones, A. Ed., *The Jerusalem Bible* Doubleday & Co., Garden City, N.Y. 1966 Mark 16:14 pg 69
13 Ibid Rev. 22:2 pg 338
14 Ibid Rev. 22:3 pg 338
15 Ibid John 20:17-18 pg 151
16 Ibid Matt. 28:19 pg 45

PART I SCRIPTURE

Introduction

1 Fujita, N. *Introducing the Bible* Paulist Press, Ramsey, N.J. 1981 pg 7

2 Keller, W. *The Bible As History* Wm. Morrow & Co., Inc. New York, N.Y. 1991 pg 18

3 Meyers, C., Gen. Ed. *Women In Scripture* Houghton Mifflin Co., New York, N.Y. 2000 pg 6

4 Patriarch: one perceived to have made major contributions to the survival of a tribe; one regarded as the founder of a tribe or nation; one through whom genealogical descent is traced or recorded.

5 Septuagint: the earliest translation of the Hebrew Bible into Greek, dating from the third century B.C., so called because of the legend which claims the work was completed by seventy-two scholars in seventy-two days; from the Latin 'septuaginta' for seventy

6 Vulgate: fourth century (c383-405 A.D.) translation of the Hebrew and the Christian Bible into Latin by Jerome, based upon the Septuagint, Itala, Masoretic texts it was the 'official' version of the Scriptures for the Roman Church for centuries

OLD TESTAMENT

Covenant

1 Idolatry: originally humans adored their own created wooden carvings or stone figures. Currently, idolatry is defined as slavery to created things i.e. money, power, drugs

2 Jones, op. cit., Gen. 17:15-16 pg 19

3 Lamm, M. *Becoming A Jew* Jonathan David Publishers, Inc. Middle Village, N.Y. 1991 pg 183

4 Jones, op. cit., Gen. 17:8 pg 19

5 Ibid Gen. 17:9-14 pg 19

6 Hawkes, J. *The First Great Civilizations* Alfred A. Knopf, New York, N.Y. 1973 pg 404

7 Daniel-Rops, H. *Israel and the Ancient World* Image Books Doubleday & Co., Inc. Garden City, N.Y. 1964 pp 34-35

8 Lamm, op. cit., pg 145

9 Ibid pg 144

10 Jones, op. cit., Deut. 10:16-20 pg 200

12 Ibid 1 Peter 2:9 pg 301

Sarah

1 Jones, op. cit., Gen. 20:13 pg 23

2 Ibid Gen. 12:2 pg 15

3 Harper, J. Ed., *Great Events of Bible Times* Doubleday & Co., Inc. Garden City, N.Y. 1987 pg 21

4 Jones, op. cit., Gen. 13:9 pg 16

5 Ibid Gen. 12:12-14 pg 16

6 Ibid Gen. 21:12-13 pg 23

7 Ibid Gen. 16:2 pg 18

8 Ibid Hebrews 11:11 pg 290

9 Ibid Galatians 4:24 pg 244

10 Ibid Gen. 21:1 pg 23

Hagar

1 Jones, op. cit., Gen. 16:5 pg 18

2 Ibid Gen. 16:6 pg 18

3 Ibid Gen. 16:10-11 pg 18

4 Ibid Gen. 25:12-18 pg 28

5 Mahmud, S. *A Short History of Islam* Oxford University Press, Pakiston 1988 pp 12-13

6 Ibid pg 5

7 Deen, E. *All the Women of the Bible* Harper & Bros., Publishers, New York, N.Y. 1955 pp 265-266

8 Speight, R. *God Is One The Way of Islam* Friendship Press, New York, N.Y. 1989 pg 2

9 John Paul II *Crossing the Threshold of Hope* Alfred A. Knopf New York, N.Y. 1994 pg 101

Rebekah

1 Jones, op. cit., Gen. 24:1-22 pg 26
2 Ibid Gen. 24:67 pg 28
3 Ibid Gen. 25:23 pp 28-29

Leah and Rachel

1 Jones, op. cit., Gen. 29:16 pg 23
2 Ibid Gen. 30:14-21 pg 34
3 Keller, op. cit. pg 68
4 Jones, op. cit., Gen. 35:2-5 pg 40

Jochebed and Zipporah

1 Jones, op. cit., Ex. 2:10 pg 61
2 Ibid Ex. 2:11-14 pg 61
3 Ibid Ex. 3:7-15 pg 62
4 Ibid Ex. 4:1-17 pg 63
5 Ibid Ex. 4:24-26 pg 64

Miriam

1 Jones, op. cit., Num. 12:8 pg 158
2 Deen, op. cit., pg 59
3 Moran, S. *A Woman for All Seasons* Twenty-third Publications, Mystic, Ct. 1993 pg 12
4 Jones, op. cit., Mic. 6:4 pg 1304

Rahab

1 Deen, op. cit., pg 67
2 Jones, op. cit., Joshua 2:2 pg212

3 Ibid Joshua 2:8-21 pg 232
4 Ibid Joshua 6:25 pg 236

Deborah

1 Jones, op. cit., Judges 4:9-10 pg 264
2 Ibid 1 Samuel 3:1-3 pg 298

Naomi and Ruth

1 Jones. op. cit., Ruth 1:1 pg 290
2 Ibid Judges 21:25 pg 289
3 Ibid Ruth 1:16-17 pg 290
4 Glean: during harvest-time, the poor were allowed to follow the reapers in the fields collecting any un-harvested grain and keep it for their own food
5 Jones, op. cit., Ruth 2:2-3 pf 291
6 Ibid Ruth 2:6 pg 291
7 Ibid Ruth 3:9 pg 292
8 Ibid Ruth 4:15-16 pg 293
9 Ibid Ruth 4:11 pg 293

Hannah

1 Jones, op. cit., 1 Samuel 1:14 pg 295
2 Ibid 1 Samuel 1:15 pg 295

Israelite Kings

1 Jones, op. cit., 1 Samuel 9:10 pg 303
2 Ibid 1 Samuel 9:1 pg 303
3 Ibid 1 Samuel 12:20-25 pg 306

4 Ibid 1 Samuel 16:1 pg 312
5 Ibid 2 Samuel 7:12-16 pg 336
6 Keller, op. cit., pg 188
7 Jones, op. cit., Gen. 17:2 pg 19

Huldah

1 Jones, op. cit., 2 Kings 22:8 pg 420
2 Ibid 2 Kings 22:14-20 pp 420-421
3 Ibid 2 Kings 23:25 pg 422
4 Swidler, L. *Biblical Affirmation of Women* The Westminster Press, Phila., Pa. 1979 pg 82
5 Libreria Editric Vaticana *Catechism of the Catholic Church* St. Paul Books and Media 1994 #120 pg 34
6 Canon: rule of belief or conduct; a formal law of the Church; Canon of Scripture: those books of Scripture considered to be true and inspired

YHWH

1 Estes, PhD. C.P. *Women Who Run With the Wolves* Ballantine Books, New York, N.Y. pg 338
2 Jones, op. cit., Gen. 4:1 pg 8
3 Eliade, N. *The Sacred and the Profane* Harcourt, Brace and World, Inc. New York, N.Y. 1959 pg 144
4 Swidler, L. *Biblical Affirmations of Women* The Westminster Press, Philadelphia, PA 1979 pg 22
5 Ling, T. *A History of Religion East and West* Harper & Row, New York, N.Y. 1970 pg 27
6 Ibid pg 107
7 Hultkrantz, A. *The Religions of the American Indians* University of California Press, Berkeley, Los Angeles, CA 1979
8 Lapp, P.W. *Biblical Archaelogy and History* The Worl Publishing Co., Cleveland, OH 1969

9 Jones, op. cit., Gen. 17:2 pg 19
10 Ibid Joseph 24:2-6 pg 257
11 Ibid Exodus 3:14 pg 62
12 Ibid Isaiah 43:11 pg 1033
13 Ibid Gen. 15:18 pg 18
14 Ibid Exodus 3:3 pg 62
15 Ibid Exodus 19:16 pg 80
16 Ibid Joshua 24:2-4 pg 257
17 Ibid Gen. 14-20 pg 17
18 Arberry, A. *The Koran Interpreted* MacMillan Publishing Co., Inc. New York, N.Y. 1974 pg 981
19 Jones, op. cit., Isaiah 42:14 pg 1031
20 Ibid Isaiah 46:3 pg 1038
21 Ibid Isaiah 66:13 pg 1066
22 Ibid Wisdom 7:25 pg 884
23 Ibid Hosea 11:5 pg 1268

NEW TESTAMENT

Jesus' Mandate

1 Swidler, op. cit., pg 14
2 Jones, op. cit., Gen. 18:1-3 pg 20
3 Ibid Galatians 4:5 pg 243
4 Ibid Leviticus 12:1-8 pg 118
5 Ibid Acts 11:10 pg 170
6 Amniotic Fluid: the fluid that fills the fetal membranes during pregnancy, It is composed of water, salts and albumin (protein). It's chief function is the protection of the fetus.
7 Jones, op. cit., Deut. 6:13 pg 195
8 Ibid Luke 9:52-56 pg 87
9 Ibid John 4:4-42 pp 119-120
10 Ibid John 4:24 pg 120

11 Smith, Rev. S.B., DD & DeLigney, F., S.J. *The Teachings of the Holy Catholic Church* The Office of Catholic Publications, 14 Barclay St., New York, N.Y. 1886 pg 167
12 Jones, op. cit., Luke 22:41-45 pg 107
13 Ibid John 7:1-15 pp 126-128

Mary of Magdala

1 Cotterell, A. *The Encyclopedia of Mythology* Anness Publishing Limited Hermes House 88-89 Blackfriars Rd., London SE1 8HA pg 181
2 Picknett, L. & Prince, C. *The Templar Revelation* Touchstone 1230 Avenue of the Americas New York, N.Y. 1997 pg 71
3 Begg, E. *The Cult of the Black Virgin* Arkana, London, 1985 pg 99
4 The Church frequently cites the Biblical verse from the Song of Songs 1:5 "I am black but I am beautiful" as allegory relating to the Black Madonna. Some icons were carved in ebony to produce a Black Madonna. According to some speculation the blackness of the icons is considered to be a sign of hermetic knowledge and power:
5 Picknett op. cit., pg 79
6 Ibid pg 248
7 In the Gospel of John, Mary of Magdala is listed following Mary, the Mother of Jesus and his aunt at the cross.
8 Jones, op. cit., Mark 15:40-41 pg 68
9 Ibid Matthew 26:55-56 pg 44
10 Ibid Luke 23:55 pg 110
11 Ibid Luke 7:36 pg 82
12 Galbati, Msgr. E. *Il Vangelo Di Gesu* Instituto S. Gaetano, Vicenza, Italia 1970 pg 123
13 Passover: seven days of unleavened bread usually 15-22 Nisan(April) commemorated departure from Egypt (Ex12:1-51, Lev. 23:10-12) barley harvest
Pentecost:seven weeks after Passover during Sivan(June) also called Feast of Weeks commemorated Decalogue on Mt. Sinai (Lev. 23, Ex. 23, Deut. 26) wheat harvest

Feast of Tabernacles six months after Passover during Bul(Nov) also called Feasts of Booths commemorated Israel's trials in the desert. (Lev.24) plow and sow wheat and barley

Hanukka also called Feasts of Lights during Chisleu (Dec)commemorated reconsecration of Temple (Macc4:52-59) winter began

Feast of Atonement also called YomKippor during tenth of Tishri (Oct) only day of the year when the high priest entered the Holy of Holies a day of fasting and penance (Lev.16)

Feast of Trumpets during Tishri (Oct) the civil New Year(Nu29:1)

Feast of Purim during Adar (Mar) commemorated Jewish deliverance from massacre planned by Hamam (Esther 3:7-9,21-24) the almond trees blossom

14 Jones, op. cit., John 2:13 pg 116
15 Ibid Mark 14:1-2 pg 64
16 Ibid Luke 4:33-37 pg 77
17 Libreria Editric Vaticana op cit #1576 pg 394
18 Jones op. cit., Hebrews 7:1-2 pg 285

Paul

1 Buckmaster, H. Paul. *A Man Who Changed the World* McGraw-Hill, New York, N.Y. 1965 pg 37
2 Jones, op. cit., Phillipians 3:6-7 pg 254
3 Ibid Acts 7:59 pg 165
4 Ibid Acts 8:1-3 pg 165
5 Ibid Acts 9:1-19 pg 167; Acts 22:1-11 pp 185-186; Acts 26:1-22 pg 190
6 Henceforth, Saul will be called Paul
7 Jones op. cit., Acts 22:3-5 pg 185
8 Ibid Romans 7:1-4 pg 203
9 Ibid Galatians 3:28-29 pg 243
10 Ibid Luke 8:40-56 pp 84-85
11 Ibid Luke 13: 10-13 pg 93
12 Ibid Luke 4:38-39 pg 77

13 Ibid Luke 7:36-50 pp 82-83
14 Ibid Luke 7:11-17 pg 81

Lydia

1 Jones, op. cit., Acts 16:11-15 pg 177

Damaris

1 Jones op. cit., Acts 17:34 pg 180

Priscilla

1 Jones, op. cit., Acts 18:24-28 pg 181
2 Ibid 1 Corinthians 16:19 pg 229
3 Ibid Romans 16:3-4 pg 212
4 Meyers, op. cit., pg 137

Phoebe

1 Jones, op. cit., 1 Timothy 3:8-12 pg 269
2 Morris, J. *The Lady Was a Bishop* The MacMillan Co., New York, N.Y. 1973 pg 120
3 Van Doornik, J. & Van de Lisdonk *A Handbook of the Catholic Faith* Image Books, Garden City, N.Y. Sept, 1956 pg 323

Chloe

1 Jones, op. cit., 1 Corinthians 1:1 pg 214

Junia

1 Jones, op. cit., Romans 16:7-8 pg 212
2 Ibid 1 Corinthians 1:1 pg 214
3 Ibid Acts 2:1 pg 257
4 King, U. Ed., *Women in the World's Religions Past & Present* Paragon House, New York, N.Y. 1985 pg 54
5 Murphy, C. *Women in the Bible* The Atlantic Monthly Vol. 272, Num. 22, August 1993 pp 39-40
6 Libreria Editric Vaticana op. cit. #1087 pg 283
7 Jones, op. cit., Ephesians 4:3-6 pg 248

What Is an Apostle? What Is a Priest? Can Women Fulfill the Role?

1 Jones, op. cit., Acts 1:21-22 pg 157
2 McKenzie, S.J.J. *Dictionary of the Bible* Geoffrey Chapman, London 1966 pg 47
3 Jones, op. cit., Matt. 10:1-16 pp 16-17; Luke 9:1-6 pg 85; Mark 10:41-45 pg 60
4 Ibid Mark 16:14-18 pg 69
5 Ibid Matthew 28:16-20 pp 4-45
6 Ibid Acts 1:15-26 pg 157
7 Ibid Luke 8:1-3 pg 157
8 Ibid Luke 23:49 pg 109
9 Ibid Luke 23:55-56 pg 110
10 Ibid Luke 24:8 pg 110
11 Ibid Matthew 27:55-56 pp 43-44
12 Ibid Mark 15:41 pg 68
13 Ibid Matthew 28:9-10 pg 44
14 Ibid Matthew 10:1-16 pp 6-17
15 Ibid Luke 9:1-6 pg 85
16 Broderick, M.A., R. Ed. *The New American Bible* Catholic Publishers, inc. Nashville, Tenn. 1971 Matt 10:9-10 pg 1081
17 Jesus commissioned the Samaritan Woman who went into town and brought the inhabitants to meet with Jesus

18 Jones, op. cit., John 13:1-20 pp 138-139

19 Ibid John 13:16 pg 139

20 Ibid Matthew 20:20-28 pg 31

21 Ibid Matthew 20:20-28 pg 31; Mark 9:33-37 pg 58; Luke 9:46-48 pg 87

22 Ibid Matthew 27:55-56 pp 43-44

23 Ibid Mark 15:40-41 pg 68

24 Ibid Luke 8:1-3 pg 83

25 Ibid Acts 4:32-35 pg 161

26 Ibid John 12:6-7 pg 136

27 Ibid Matthew 5:25 pg 10

28 Ibid Matthew 5:41 pg 11

29 Ibid Matthew 5:44 pg 11

30 Ibid Matthew 9:19 pg 30; Matthew 22:39 pg 34

31 Ibid John 15:12 pg42

32 Mary, mother of Jesus, was of the tribe of Aaron, priestly tribe. So, Jesus inherited His kingship through Joseph who was of David's tirbe, but His priesthood from Mary, who was of Aaron's tribe

33 Jones, op. cit., Matthew 8:4 pg 14; Luke 5:14 pg 79

34 Ibid Matthew 12:1-8 pg 19; Luke 6:1-5 pg 79

35 Jones, op. cit., Romans 16:1 pg 212

36 Ibid 1 Timothy 3:11 pg 269

37 Ibid Romans 16:1-16 pg 212

38 Daughters of St. Paul *The Vatican II Weekday Missal* Published by the Daughters of St. Paul, Boston, Mass. 1975 pg 884

PART II TRADITION

Introduction

1 Novak, P. *The World's Wisdom* Harper Collins Publishers, New York, N.Y. 1994 pg 213

2 Greenwood, Rev. J., Ed. *A Handbook of the Catholic Faith* Image Books, Doubleday & Co., Inc. Garden City, N.Y. 1956 pg 151

3 Note here the overlap and inter-dependency of Tradition and Magisterium. Church Councils, theologians, Doctors of the Church also contribute to the Magisterium
4 Jones, op. cit., Luke 10:42 pg 89

Religious Symbols

1 Webster *Dictionary for Everyday Use* P.S.I. Associates, Inc. Miami, Fla. 1986
2 Campbell, J. *The Masks of God: Primitive Mythology* The Viking Press, New York, N.Y. 1959 pg 119
3 Ibid pg 257
4 Middleton, J. Ed. *Gods and Rituals* The Natural History Press, Garden City, N.Y. 1967 pg 129
5 Charbonneau, L. *Christ the Hunter and the Hunted* Parabola Vol. XVI Num. 2 May 1991 pp 23-25
6 Campbell, op. cit., pg 64
7 Jones, op. cit., Gen. 1:2 pg5

Eucharist

2 Jones, op. cit., 1Kings 8:63 pg 373
3 Ibid Genesis 4:1-6 pg 8
4 Visser, M. *The Rituals of Dinner* Grove Weidenfeld, New York, N.Y. pg 35
5 Jones, op. cit., John 15:5-17 pg 142
6 Ibid Peter 2:9 pg 301
7 Ibid Matthew 28:19 pg 45
8 Ibid Acts 2:4 pg 157
9 Ibid Isaiah 45:15 pg 1037
10 Ibid Isaiah 53:5 pg 1049

Woman in Church Tradition

1 Jones, op. cit., Nahum 3:4 pg 1310
2 Swidler, L. op. cit., pg 158
3 Morris, J. *The Lady Was a Bishop* The MacMillan Co., New York, N.Y. 1973 pg XI
4 Herberman, C.G., Ed. *Catholic Encyclopedia* Robert Appleton Co., New York, N.Y. 1911 Vol 1 pg 9
5 Loret, P. *The Story of the Mass* Liguori Publications, Li-guori, MO. 1982 pg 33
6 Reuther, R.R. *Womanguides* Beacon Press, Boston, MA. 1985 pg 80
7 Jones, op. cit., Acts 21:9-10 pg 184
8 McNamara, J. *Sisters in Arms* Harvard University Press, Cambridge, MA 1996 pg 30
9 Pagels, E. *Adam, Ever, and the Serpent* Random House, New York, N.Y. 1988 pg 58
10 Murphy, C. op. cit., pp 39-64
11 Morris, J. op. cit., pg 8
12 Ibid pg 6
13 Pagels, E. *The Gnostic Gospels* Random House, New York, N.Y. 1979 pg 42
14 Ibid pg 42
15 McNamara, op. cit., pg 40
16 Ibid pg 42
17 Reuther, R.R. *Women-Church* Harper & Row, Publishers, San Francisco, CA 1985 pg 284
18 Harkness, G. *Women in Church and Society* Abingdon Press, New York, N.Y. 1972 pg 73
19 This title is not to be confused with the title 'episcopissa' the term used to describe the wife of a bishop
20 Morris, J. op. cit. Appendix V, Ordination of Abbesses
21 Lasance, Rev. F. *The New Roman Missal* Benziger Bros., Inc., New York, N.Y. 1937 pp 63-65
22 McNamara, op. cit., pg 116
23 Ibid pg 196

24 Ibid pg 84
25 Ibid pg 57
26 Sellner, E. *Wisdom of the Celtic Saints* Ave Maria Press, Notre Dame, Ind. 1993 pg 27
27 Ibid pg 197
28 Herberman, op. cit., pg 9
29 Bede *Ecclesiastical History of the English Nation* Translated by J. Stevens 1723 pg 202
30 Chernow, B. & Vallasa, G. *The Columbia Encyclopedia* Fifth Edition Columbia University Press, New York, N.Y. 1993 pg 861
31 Herberman, op. cit., pg 9
32 ibid pg 9
33 McNamara, op. cit., pg 197
34 Ibid pg 224
35 Fernandez, Armesti *Millennium* Charles Scribner's Son, New York, N.Y. 1995 pp 57-59
36 McNamara, op. cit., pg 222
37 Morris, op. cit., pg 141
38 Tuchman, B. *A Distant Mirror* Alfred A. Knopf, New York, N.Y. 1978 pg 211
39 Brooten, B. Junia...*Outstanding Among the Apostles* in Leonard & Arlene Swidler, eds. *Women Priests: A Catholic Commentary on the Vatican Declaration* Paulist Press, N.Y. 1977 pp141-144
40 King, op. cit., pg 54
41 Jones, op. cit., Romans 16:7-8 pg 212
42 Givry, G. *The Illustrated Anthology of Sorcery, Magic and Alchemy* Causeway Books, New York, N.Y. 1973 pg 199
43 Tuchman, B. op. cit., pg 123
44 Jones, op. cit., Acts 9:36-43 pg 168
45 Lerner, G. *The Creation of Feminist Consciousness* Oxford University Press, New York, N.Y. 1993 pg 20
46 Weaver, M. *New Catholic Women* Harper & Row, San Francisco, CA 1985 pp 32-33
47 Ibid pg 34

48 *Vatican Study Helped Anglican Decision to Ordain Women* National Catholic Reporter, Kansas City, MO Vol 30, Num.22 April 1, 1994

49 Steinfels, P. *Vatican Says Ban On Women as Priests Is 'Infallible Doctrine'* New York Times, Vol 27 Num. 50250 Nov. 19, 1995 pg 1

PART III MAGISTERIUM

Introduction

1 Jones, op. cit., Mark 16:14-20 pg 69
2 Jones, op. cit., Matthew,28:16-20 pg 45
3 Ibid Luke 24:19-29 pg 151
4 Ibid John 20:19-29 pg 151
5 Ibid Acts 1:6-11 pg 156
6 Libreria Editrice Vaticana op. cit., #91 pg 28; #92 pg28
7 John Paul II *Sacerdotalis Ordinatio*

Power of the Keys

1 Jones, op. cit., Matthew 16:16-17 pg 26
2 Ibid Matthew 16:19 pg 26
3 Libreria Editrice Vaticana op. cit., #552 pg 141
4 Jones op. cit., Matthew 28:20 pg 45
5 Libreria Editrice Vaticana op. cit., #553 pg 142
6 Jones op. cit., John 21:1-17 pg 152
7 Ibid Acts 4:32 pg 161
8 Libreria Editrice Vaticana op. cit., #85 pg 27
9 Jones, op. cit., Matthew 15:25-28 pg 25
10 Pagels, E. op. cit., pg 105
11 Gibbon, E. *The Decline and Fall of the Roman Empire* Washington Square Press, inc. New York, N.Y. 1962 (Abr. D.M. Low) Vol 1 pg 398

12 Some scholars maintain that Constantine was baptized upon his death bed.

13 Gibbon, op. cit., pg 400

14 Ibid pg 400

15 Pagels, E. *Adam, Eve and the Serpent* Random House, New York, N.Y. 1988 pg 124

16 Gibbon, op. cit., pp 395-396

Freedom Lost

1 Jones, op. cit., Romans 7:6 pg 203

2 Adversus Haereses (Against Heresies) 3.4.1

3 Pagels, E. *The Gnostic Gospels* Random House, New York, N.Y. 1979 pg 105

4 A tribunal formed to investigate, convict and condemn heretics. There were three: Medieval, established by Gregory IX; the Spanish of Ferdinand and Isabel, approved by Sixtus IV; Congregation of the Holy Office, founded by Paul III

Eucharist

1 Vatican II Lumen Gentium 21 Nov 1964

2 Vatican II Sacrosanctum Concilium 4 Dec 1963 #2

3 Pagels, E. *The Gnostic Gospels* Random House, New York, N.Y. 1979 pg 105

4 Gibbon, op. cit., pg 380

5 Loret, P. op. cit., pp 76-77

6 Ibid pg 85

7 Flannery, O.P., A, Ed. *Vatican Council II* Eerdmann's Publishing Co., Grand Rapids, MI 1992 pg 1

8 Jones, op. cit., Luke 24:13-35 pp 110-111

Anti-Semitism

1 Jones, op. cit., John 20:19 pg 151
2 Fujita, op. cit., pg 141
3 Ignatius, Letter to the magnesians
4 Calendar of Jewish Persecutions
5 Sermon of John Chrysostom quoted in Dixon, M. pg 80
6 Hill garth, J. N. *The Spanish Kingdoms 1250-1516* Clarendon Press, Oxford, England 1978 pg 133
7 Ibid pg 142
8 Ibid pg 452
9 Galileo's conviction was annulled at the request of John Paul II three centuries after the fact
10 Oberman, H. A. *Luther* Image Books, New York, N.Y. 1992 pg 290
11 *St. Andrew's Daily Missal* E.M. Lohmann, St. Paul, MI 1945 pg 566
12 Jones, op. cit., Romans, 9:4-5 pp 205-206
13 Cornwell, J. *Hitler's Pope The Secret History of Pius XII* Viking Penguin, N.Y. 1999 Preface

Slavery

1 Josephus, Ant. XII, 11.3
2 Jones, op. cit., Gen. 17:23-27 pg 20
3 Ibid Exodus 21:1-11 pg 82
4 Ibid James 2:1 pg 296
5 Ibid Peter 2:16-19 pg 301
6 Ibid Romans 7:6 pg 203
7 Ibid Acts 18:12-17 pg 180
8 Ibid Ephesians 6:9 pg 250
9 Ibid Matthew 22:21-22 pg 34
10 Ibid Galatians 3:27-29 pg 243

11 Jackson, D.D., LL.D., Samuel, Editor in Chief *The New SchaffHerzog Religious Encyclopedia* Baker Book House, Grand Rapids, MI 1977 pg 451

12 Anathema: severe ecclesiastical penalty which excludes one from participation in the sacraments. Absolution cannot be granted except by the Pope or his authorized designee.

13 Jones, op. cit., Ephesians 6:5 pg 250

14 The name given by Erasmus to the unknown author of a commentary on the Epistles of St. Paul composed between 370-384 A.D.

15 Editorial Staff Catholic University of America, Wash., D.C., *New Catholic Encyclopedia* McGraw Hill Book Co., New York, N.Y. 1967 pp 282-287

16 Vatican II, Gaudium et Spes, 7 December 1965 #29 (929)

Woman in Magisterium

1 Harkness, op. cit., pg 73

2 Ibid pg 73

3 Canon 26, 441 A.D.

4 Swidler, L. *Biblical Affirmation of Women* The Westminster Press, Philadelphia, PA. 1979 pg 314

5 Swidler, L. & Swidler, A., Eds. *Women Priests* Paulist Press, New York, N.Y. 1977 pg 141

6 Swidler. L. op. cit., pg 104

7 McNamara, op. cit., pg 84

8 cans. 34; q.5, C.11

9 L'Abbe, Droit Canon, Paris 1859. Vol. 2 Col. 75

10 Pegis, A.D. Ed. *Basic Writings of St. Thomas Aquinas* Random House, New York, N.Y. 1945 pg 880

11 Ibid Q92 ART I

12 John Paul II *Crossing the Threshold of Hope* Alfred A. Knopf, New York, N.Y. 1994 pg 217

CONCLUSION

1 Editorial Staff Catholic University of America, op. cit., Vol 4 pp 939-946
2 Dogma: refers to those elements of faith or morals pronounced by the Church as requiring belief by all of the faithful
3 Editorial Staff Catholic University of America, op. cit., Vol 4 pp 939-946
4 Ibid pp 939-946
5 Jones, op. cit., James 2:9 pg 296
6 Libreria Editrice Vaticana op. cit., pg 395 #1582
7 Ibid pg 398 #1593
8 Kung, H. *On Being a Christian* Doubleday & Co., Inc. Garden City, N.Y. 1976 pg 527
9 Pomfret, J. *Disaffected Catholics Call on Church to Open Up to Modern Age* International Herald Tribune September 15, 1995 pg 2
10 Call to Action News, Chicago, IL Spring 1996, Vol 18, Num.1 pg 4
11 Eckholm, E. New York Times May 30, 1994 pg 1
12 Vatican City, VIS *The Long Island Catholic* Vol 34 Num 16 26 July 1995
13 Bohlen, C. *Pope Calls for an End to Discrimination Against Women* New York Times, 11/July/1995 pg A11
14 John Paul II op. cit., pg 47
15 Jones, op. cit., Ephesians 2:19-22 pg 248
16 Advent: the term applies to the liturgical penitential season of anticipation which precedes the Feast of Christmas (approximately four weeks)
17 Jones, op. cit., Luke 1:26-38 pg 71
18 Ibid Luke 10:42 pg 89
19 Ibid Romans 9:1-5 pp 205-206

ABOUT THE AUTHOR

During her professional career, Sally served as Nurse Educator and as Director of Nursing in acute and long term care facilities. As a consultant, Sally lectured and conducted seminars on curriculum development, management, and leadership development in many Eastern States and in the U.S. Virgin Islands.

Published in several professional journals, author of "A Woman for All Seasons," Sally has continued to write since her retirement from Nursing Practice, and has lectured on Marian and Scriptural themes in South Carolina, New Jersey, and New York.

Printed in the United States
19888LVS00006B/217-276